GREAT LANDSCAPE
EVERGREENS

VINCENT A. SIMEONE

{ *Photography by Bruce Curtis, Foreword by A. Wayne Cahilly, Preface by Margret Roach* }

 Ball Publishing | Batavia, Illinois

Ball Publishing
P.O. Box 9
335 N. River St.
Batavia, IL 60510
www.ballpublishing.com

ISBN 978-1-883052-63-8

Library of Congress Cataloging-in-Publication Data

Simeone, Vincent A.
  Great landscape evergreens / Vincent A. Simeone ; photography by Bruce
Curtis ; preface by Margaret Roach ; foreword by A. Wayne Cahilly.
      p. cm.
  Includes bibliographical references and index.
  ISBN 978-1-883052-63-8 (hardcover : alk. paper)
  1. Ornamental evergreens. 2. Landscape gardening. I. Curtis, Bruce,
1944- II. Title.

SB435.S4835 2008
635.9'7715--dc22
                              2007043443

Printed and bound in China by Imago.
9 8 7 6 5 4 3 2 1   08 09 10 11 12 13 14

Special Thanks

This book is dedicated to my family, whose encouragement and untiring support has enabled me to flourish as a person. Their understanding during the long hours and late nights has been inspirational. Special thanks to my wife, Gloria, who has supported me every step of the way.

Assorted evergreens in the landscape

Assorted conifers in the landscape

} "Give me a land of boughs in leaf,

A land of trees that stand;

Where trees are fallen there is grief;

I love no leafless land."

— **A.E. Housman**

Table of Contents

Acknowledgments

The photographs for this book were taken at Bayard Cutting Arboretum, Oakdale, New York; Bethpage State Park, Bethpage, New York; Griffith Nursery, Watkinsville, Georgia; Hofstra Arboretum, Hempstead, New York; New York Botanical Garden, Bronx, New York; the garden of Bruce and Paula Rice, Lloyd Harbor, New York; Planting Fields Arboretum State Historic Park, Oyster Bay, New York; Sonnenberg Gardens, Canandaigua, New York; the garden of Marianne and Bruce Feller, Village of Oldfield, New York; Walt Disney World, Orlando, Florida; Penn State University, University Park, Pennsylvania; Morton Arboretum, Lisle, Illinois; Toronto Music Garden, Toronto, Ontario, Canada; Mottisfont Abbey, Romsey, Hampshire, England; and Weihenstephan Gardens, Freising, Germany. Also, I would like to extend my sincere gratitude to the collaborators on this book: Bruce Curtis, Wayne Cahilly, Margaret Roach, Tim Smalley, and Gloria Simeone.

6/5/09

to the inspired Gardener!

the best is yet to come!

Vinnie Simeone

About This Book

Today, more than ever, homeowners desire privacy in their garden. Conifers, broadleaf evergreens, and even select deciduous trees and shrubs offer great structure and physical presence in the landscape. With increased pest problems affecting popular favorites such as Canadian hemlock and the overuse of other common evergreens, such as arborvitae, juniper, and euonymus, we crave something other than what is repeatedly dangled in front of us. Many species of conifers and broadleaf evergreens can adapt to various environmental conditions while offering great beauty and function in the landscape.

This book presents many choice and select evergreens and deciduous woody plants that are ideal as screens and hedges. It celebrates some old favorites and their unique varieties and also highlights many unknown but worthy species that can be incorporated into the garden. Important information on each plant species—including ornamental value, landscape value, care and culture, and landscape design tips—are also featured in this book.

Great Landscape Evergreens challenges the reader to think outside the box and explore the wonderful world of gardening. Horticulture is a continuous journey motivating us to explore new avenues as it evolves, revealing endless, new possibilities. For me the journey continues to be an inspiring one.

Foreword

American gardens lack structure.

A bold statement, you may say, and you may doubt its accuracy, as well, but hear me out. What gives structure to a garden? Trees, yes; shrubs, yes, of course; but the defining element that controls the experience within the garden and guides and enhances the view are plants that screen. American residential gardens spill over their edges from yard to yard, from view to view, with little forethought given to maximizing the garden space and minimizing distractions. Perhaps a past fling at hemlock or privet hedging dangles at the edges of the yard, but what of plants that provide color, texture, fruit, flowers; attract wildlife; grow in such a way as to do the desired job; and live in the conditions with which you have to work?

This book is about screening: screening with plants, good plants and great plants creatively used in ways that enhance the garden by providing more than a foil for perennials. It is about creating vision, controlling experiences, and gardening. Review the plants listed here and compare them to your site. How much depth do you have to work with at the edges or in creating interior garden spaces? Do you like the rigid, formal appearance of vertical evergreens standing shoulder to shoulder or plants that are loose and free flowing? Bold, colored foliage, such as that of *Aucuba japonica*, can brighten a protected corner by simply being there. *Myrica pensylvanica* is native and deciduous, while *Cedrus atlantica* 'Glauca' reaches 80 ft. in height and equal in width, enough to screen nearly anything.

Recently, gardeners have lamented the loss of hemlock as a screening plant. Insect pests have relegated this once-ubiquitous hedging plant to the bargain basement sales lot of the local nurseries—and to the frustration list of those gardeners whose yards are surrounded by them. Insect and disease resistance is a prime consideration given to the plants that have been included in this book. Other plants have bad habits, such as producing acres of seedlings within moments of planting; those plants do not appear here. From big and bold evergreen trees to dainty foreground shrubs, this book provides alternatives to the troublesome screening plants of the past and presents a range of new opportunities if only the gardener will be brave.

Vincent Simeone has provided us with a wealth of knowledge acquired through working with these plants. As the director of Planting Fields Arboretum, Vinnie has had ample opportunity to see plants develop into mature form while being used to enclose garden spaces and to distract from potentially unsightly views. Vinnie has lectured and taught extensively on his favorite subject, trees and shrubs, and has invested much of himself and his understanding of woody plants in this volume.

Most gardeners' bookshelves possess some books that should be considered suspect, having been written by people who lack sufficient experience to speak as experts on their chosen subject. This book is well researched, authoritative, and written by one who practices what he has recommended. This book is not fluff; it's the meat and potatoes required to give a residential garden structure, definition; and enclosure; it is a keeper.

A. Wayne Cahilly
Horticulturist
The New York Botanical Garden

Preface

I had my unintentional introduction to woody plants at Planting Fields Arboretum on Long Island in the early 1970s. I admit that I wasn't there for the horticulture or landscape architecture, but more the chance for a game of Frisbee on the parklike former estate's great expanse of lawn. Even to my teenage eyes, however, the place made an impression, and I came away a plant person, charmed by the shapes and textures and personalities of specimens like the Sargent weeping hemlock, whose formal name, *Tsuga canadensis* 'Sargentii', was the first botanical Latin I ever memorized.

Fast forward about two decades to a spring day in 1993: By then I knew a lot about plants—or thought I did. Not far from where those imposing weeping hemlocks still grew, I was introduced to Vincent Simeone, Planting Fields' newly hired curator of plant collections. My first impression: How could someone so young possibly tackle such a vast job, overseeing a collection of ten thousand woody plants on 409 acres? It took just that first walk on the grounds with Vinnie for me to know the answer.

If the woody plant world could speak up and nominate its own spokesperson, Vinnie would be it. It doesn't hurt, either, that Vinnie is a natural teacher, and despite our backwards age equation, I immediately found myself in the role of student from that very first day. I learned about disease-resistant cultivars of elm; exceptional trees, like *Stewartia*, with not just one but multiple seasons of interest; and how to rejuvenate leggy, overgrown rhododendron (or when, instead, to face it that a woody plant is just too far gone and just to start over). The lessons were each geared to real issues that homeowners with gardens face, and were (and still are) delivered patiently without a hint of talking down or any details left out.

Those are the same qualities that make Vinnie's latest book, *Great Landscape Evergreens*, a valuable addition to my garden bookshelf. Like the three volumes that preceded it in his woody plant gardening series, this book helps beginning and experienced gardeners alike make the best possible choices about the plants they invest in, and teaches us to care for them as well as Vinnie and his team care for the collection at Planting Fields. Specifically, this volume answers one of the most challenging and common questions each of us has in making a garden: how to block out unwanted views, whether merely the compost heap or a whole roadside boundary.

Sadly, various old standbys, including Canadian hemlock, just don't work anymore, for reasons of pests or diseases. Plants like western red cedar (*Thuja plicata*) and *Cryptomeria japonica* and evergreen viburnums are much better choices for contemporary landscapes.

But don't take my word for it. Take Vinnie's, as I have been privileged to do so many times.

Margaret Roach
Editorial Director
Martha Stewart Living

A Brief Introduction to Evergreens

Evergreens are the foundation of any well-designed garden. They act as the landscape cornerstone on which a great garden is built. With their wonderful textures, colors, and forms, evergreens offer interest all four seasons of the year. Another of the most valuable qualities of evergreens is their great diversity of landscape applications. Evergreens can be used as screens, hedges, groupings, foundation plantings, or as simple single specimens.

My true appreciation for evergreens was solidified during a garden tour of England when I visited two great gardens, Wisley Gardens and the garden of Sir Harold Hillier. They are easily two of the most magnificent and comprehensive collections of woody plants in the world. The towering spruces, firs, and pines, along with the understory of massive rhododendrons, were breathtaking. Since then I have taken closer notice of evergreens and continuously seek them out in the garden to marvel at their beauty and versatility.

Over the past decade or so, there has been a growing interest in evergreens and their function as hedges and screens. I suppose one motivation for this could be our ever-growing desire for privacy, as new housing continues to be developed, but there are other reasons, as well. I believe our yearning for a diverse palette of evergreens

© Vincent A. Simeone

Hemlock with woolly adelgid

is directly linked to past tribulations. For example, over the past two decades, one of our great American natives, Canadian hemlock (*Tsuga canadensis*), has been seriously threatened by an insect known as the woolly adelgid. This destructive pest is equipped with a fuzzy protective shield as it colonizes entire branches of trees, eventually killing its hosts. Although this insect can be managed with regular monitoring and occasional pesticide applications, this problem has still affected the future of hemlock as a viable landscape plant.

With the demise of Canadian hemlock and the overuse of such evergreens as American arborvitae (*Thuja occidentalis*), Colorado spruce (*Picea pungens*), and red tip photinia (*Photinia × fraseri*), to name just a few, a need for diversification was realized by the gardening world. With improved technology, plant breeding, and nursery production, the introduction and acquisition of new selections of evergreens has become much easier.

With this in mind, it is important to realize the value of evergreens in the landscape and to plan accordingly. All too often evergreens are misused, seeming to litter the poorly planned garden rather than accentuate it. Several factors need to be considered when selecting evergreens as screens or hedges. First, what is the main objective you want your evergreens to accomplish? Tall screen to hide the neighbor's garage? A low hedge to screen a pool filter or the foundation of a shed? Another important consideration when choosing evergreens is to determine what environment your plants will be growing in. What type of soil and light exposure does your garden offer? Is it a windy, hot, dry, or exposed site? Do you have well drained soil? Is the soil clay or sandy loam? Knowing the desired outcome and existing growing conditions are crucial in the decision-making process, dictating the species that are

© Bruce Curtis

Golden thread falsecypress in the landscape

most appropriate for a specific landscape project.

Other important considerations when choosing evergreens as screens or hedges are ornamental value, growth rate, and ultimate size. One of the most common miscues in the siting of evergreens in the landscape is not allowing enough room for the plant to grow. Too many landscapes are burdened with plants that outgrow their allocated space. The theory that "I'll just prune it if it gets too large" is not a sound one. Trees and shrubs planted too closely to each other or structures will require more frequent pruning and may ultimately become problematic, even with regular care. The best practice is to choose evergreens that will thrive in the soil and light conditions that are available and will be suitable for the space that is allocated.

Research the ultimate size of the various species of evergreens appropriate for your location.

THE FUNCTION OF EVERGREENS

If used correctly, evergreens offer privacy and shelter from the outside world and make us feel more secure in our living spaces. In addition, a functional hedge or screen provides structure as well as aesthetic value. In general, a good screening plant should be dense, fast growing, tolerant of pruning, and adaptable to various environmental conditions. Many gardeners prefer evergreens because they retain their leaves year round. Actually, evergreens do drop their older leaves, but the newer ones remain, so the plant is always covered with foliage.

There are two types of evergreens: broadleaf and narrow-leaved, or needled. Broadleaf evergreens typically have wide, lush leaves, while needled evergreens have very thin, fine foliage. Needled evergreens are also known as conifers, since they bear cones; examples include spruce, fir, and pine. Some conifers, such as arborvitae, falsecypress, and juniper, have smooth, scalelike leaves.

Evergreens offer various types of growth habits, textures, and colors in the landscape. Some have deep green leaves, while others display variegated, gold, or blue foliage. These rich colors seem to be most vibrant and noticeable during the cooler months of fall and winter.

While evergreens can function as a screen or hedge for privacy, they also give structure to the landscape. A strategically placed single specimen can be just as effective for aesthetic purposes as a grouping of trees.

A grouping, though, can also affect temperature. It is estimated that a properly planned coniferous screen can save up to 30% of heating costs during winter. In chapter 6 of this book, Landscaping with Screening Plants, there is detailed information on how to site and plant your evergreens to maximize their effectiveness in the landscape.

USING PLANTS AS HEDGES AND SCREENS

Screens and hedges perform many functions in the landscape. Among the most important is their ability to hide unsightly views and create sound barriers, protection from the wind, and temperature modification. They also give the landscape an enclosed or defined area. A well-designed, carefully planned hedge or screen not only is a living barrier for privacy and security, but it also provides structure and year-round interest to a garden.

A hedge is defined as a row of closely planted shrubs or low-growing trees forming a fence or boundary. Hedges can be planted in a straight line or in a staggered, random fashion, depending on the need and ultimate goal of the planting. The main difference between a formal and an informal hedge is the manner in which the plants are pruned. Formal hedges are typically sheared into tight, formal, rounded shapes or angular lines. Shearing is a type of pruning that primarily removes the top layer of foliage from the plant. This prevents plants from taking a natural form. Shearing is often done on a regular basis to maintain a dense, manicured look. When creating a clipped or

© Bruce Curtis

Formal yew hedge

© Vincent A. Simeone

Japanese holly pruned informally

An informal hedge is usually not pruned or sheared formally but, rather, is left natural to create a less restrained appearance. Essentially, an informal hedge is freer flowing. I prefer this method of hedging because it creates a more naturalistic planting and typically creates a healthier and more productive plant.

© Vincent A. Simeone

Tall screens in the landscape

A screen is very similar to a hedge, but typically it is larger and taller and, in addition to blocking unsightly views, can act as a windbreak and sound barrier. Tall screens are often kept informal because they can reach large sizes once mature. Screens are typically made up of fast-growing conifers such as spruce, fir, juniper, cypress, and arborvitae.

Please see illustrations 1 through 5 in Landscaping with Screening Plants, chapter 6, to learn more about different types of hedges and screens.

formal hedge, prune the bottom slightly wider than the top, so all the foliage receives adequate sunlight. A perfectly vertical clipping can cause the bottom portion of the plants to die out.

USING PLANT NAMES

Both scientific plant names and common names are important parts of everyday gardening life. Scientific names are written in Latin, the universal language in the horticultural world. They basically comprise a genus, also referred to as generic term, and a specific epithet. (Many varieties have additional names pinpointing types even further than species level.) Such *binomial nomenclature* is important to understand, especially when researching or purchasing plants from a local nursery or garden center. A genus is a group of closely related plants comprising one or more species. The *specific epithet* identifies the particular member of the genus, the *species*. For example, the scientific name for eastern white pine is *Pinus strobus* (genus + specific epithet).

When discussing multiple species of the same genus, it is common to use only the initial of the genus name. Here's a passage from this book's Camellias section: "There are two main species valued as garden ornamentals in America, Japanese camellia (*Camellia japonica*) and sasanqua camellia (*C. sasanqua*). These ornamental camellias are close relatives of the tea plant (*C. sinensis*), which is of course a major economic crop."

In addition to a scientific name, every plant typically has one or more common names, which often describe a notable physical or other characteristic of the plant. For example, leatherleaf viburnum (*Viburnum rhytidophyllum*) offers large, lustrous, leathery leaves all year.

Common names tend to create confusion, though. They can vary between regions, so a given plant may have multiple common names. *Thuja occidentalis*, for instance, is usually referred to as American arborvitae. It is also known as eastern arborvitae—a name that complements its close relative western arborvitae (*T. plicata*). Because of its bark and wood, *T. occidentalis* is even known as white cedar, though it's not a true cedar at all.

Conversely, a given common name may refer to several unrelated plants. Take "burning bush": it may mean certain shrubs in the genus *Euonymus* (also known as spindle tree, winged euonymus, and wahoo), the shrub *Bassia scoparia* (also firebush, fireball, Mexican fireweed, summer cypress, and belvedere), rambling tropical shrubs of the genus *Combretum* (flame creeper, flame keeper, fire vine), or the perennial herb *Dictamnus albus* (gas plant, dittany, fraxinella).

As you can see, the one scientific name, even though it's in Latin, is more reliable for finding or identifying a plant. It is important for even the casual gardener to learn both scientific and common names.

Some plant names include terms beyond the species level that are helpful to understand. A *cultivar*, also referred to as a *cultivated variety* or *garden variety*, is cultivated or selected for certain special garden qualities that are distinct from the basic species. Cultivated varieties or garden varieties typically originate in a garden and have very specific ornamental characteristics and landscape functions that are valuable in the cultivated garden. Cultivar names are capitalized and are usually surrounded by single quotation marks, or you may find the single quotes replaced by the abbreviation "cv." (for *cultivated variety*) before the name.

HARDINESS ZONE MAP

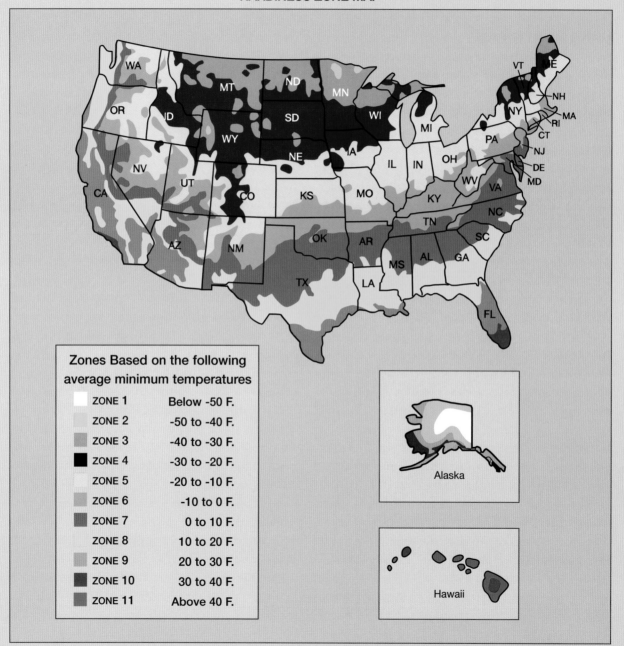

Zones Based on the following average minimum temperatures

	ZONE 1	Below -50 F.
	ZONE 2	-50 to -40 F.
	ZONE 3	-40 to -30 F.
	ZONE 4	-30 to -20 F.
	ZONE 5	-20 to -10 F.
	ZONE 6	-10 to 0 F.
	ZONE 7	0 to 10 F.
	ZONE 8	10 to 20 F.
	ZONE 9	20 to 30 F.
	ZONE 10	30 to 40 F.
	ZONE 11	Above 40 F.

Alaska

Hawaii

For example, the scientific name for gold dust plant can be written as *Aucuba japonica* 'Variegata' or *Aucuba japonica* cv. *Variegata.*

Some *trademarked* or *registered* plant names are more common and identifiable in the market than the cultivar names, and such names don't take single quotes. When trade or registered names are used in this book, the cultivated variety names follow in parentheses, as in this line from the rose discussion: "Recently, there have been several new introductions to the Knock Out series, including Pink Knock Out ('Radcon') and Blushing Knock Out ('Radyod')." You can see where these cultivar names would be less popular in commerce than the trade names.

Although the term *variety* in this book commonly designates a garden variety (cultivar), the true scientific term refers to a naturally occurring variation within a species. In a scientific name it is written in lowercase letters and without single quotations, following the abbreviation *var.* For example, *Picea glauca* var. *conica* is the scientific name for Alberta spruce. It is a naturally occurring variety with very small, dense needles and a semi-dwarf growth habit, as opposed to the species (*P. glauca*), which has large needles and develops into a larger tree.

HARDINESS ZONES

The USDA Plant Hardiness Zone Map illustrates the average minimum temperatures of the United States. The map is separated into eleven zones, with 1 representing the coldest zone, 11 the warmest. Although several environmental factors—such as heat, humidity, and rainfall—have an impact on plant adaptability, cold hardiness is one of the most important. It is important to identify the zone where you live to ensure the winter survival of the plants you select. Plants that are tender or marginally hardy in a given hardiness zone may perform poorly or die. The hardiness zone range for each plant species or variety in this book is listed within the text of each plant description.

To learn your hardiness zone, identify the area where you live on the map on page 6. There is a zone number assigned to that region. For example, the hardiness zone for Chicago is Zone 5. For exact temperature ranges within a given hardiness zone, read the zone key located below the map.

In 2006, the National Arbor Day Foundation released their own zone map, reflecting a general warming of temperatures across North America since the USDA map was released in 1990. Using fifteen years' worth of climactic data, they determined that significant portions of many states have shifted at least one full hardiness zone. While this map is not "official" for the United States, you can use as a guide it if you want to stretch your traditional zone a bit and experiment with some new plants. You can find the map at www.arborday.org/media/zones.cfm.

NATIVES VERSUS EXOTIC SPECIES

Recent debate has raised questions about the value of native species in the garden and the challenges that invasive exotic species present to our environment. The purpose of this book is to acknowledge the wonderful attributes of exceptional evergreens that can add beauty and function to the home landscape. It is not intended to alienate you from or exclude any group of plants. This book gives equal attention to worthwhile native evergreens and excellent exotics as valuable assets to American gardens. It is important to have a diverse landscape with a strong balance of natives and exotic species.

The perception that all exotic species are invasive is a false one. The key to a successful garden and healthy environment is to discourage the infiltration of invasive exotic species whenever possible and to encourage superior natives and noninvasive exotics. If we were to follow the notion that the use of all exotic species should be curtailed, we would never get to experience the wonderful assets of Oriental spruce, lacebark pine, Japanese cryptomeria, and so many other exceptional garden plants.

Conifers

Conifers are the cornerstone of the landscape and provide great beauty and function in the context of selecting a living screen. A conifer, a tree or shrub bearing cones, has thin, needlelike foliage and typically a dense habit that lends itself to making a screen or tall hedge. There are many popular conifers, as well as a few lesser-known species, that present fine-textured foliage ranging from rich green to blue-green to gold. Conifers add a unique textural quality that provides four seasons of landscape interest. Established specimens are most noticeable in the fall and winter months when the rest of the landscape is leafless.

This section describes some common, well-known plants that are ideal as screens and hedges, as well as some lesser-known, select species and varieties that deserve more consideration.

{ *Abies* spp.
Fir

Firs and spruces (*Picea* spp.) are both staples in the landscape and are valued for their versatility. Both conifers possess upright, dense, pyramidal growth habits and are quite effective in small groupings.

Firs and spruces thrive in the cooler climates and higher elevations of North America, Asia, and Europe. They both prefer well-drained, moist soil and full or partial sun.

There are about forty species of firs, which grow all over the world. In general, they are large, pyramidal evergreens that typically outgrow the small, residential landscape. Most fir species thrive in cooler, northern climates of the United States and grow too large for most residential sites. However, the white fir (*Abies concolor*) and the Momi fir

© Vincent A. Simeone

Informal planting of conifers in winter

White fir in the landscape

© Vincent A. Simeone

Soft, gray needles of white fir

© Bruce Curtis

(*A. firma*) are quite adaptable and offer exceptional merit for gardens with adequate space.

Abies concolor (white fir)

White fir is an interesting conifer with long, smooth, silvery blue needles. The slender needles and soft texture provide a graceful, bright accent in the garden. White fir, also known as concolor fir, has a tight, pyramidal growth habit when young and will eventually become tall and broad as it matures. It is a truly breathtaking sight in the winter landscape.

Like most firs, this species prefers moist, well-drained soil and full sun or partial shade. However, white fir is relatively easy to grow and will adapt to various landscape situations. In general it is more tolerant of heat and humidity than other species of fir. White fir can grow 30–50 ft. or more in height with about half the spread and should be sited where it will have adequate room to grow.

White fir is useful as a single specimen or in a grouping. It can be used as a tall screen to block an unsightly view or soften an architectural feature. The silver foliage will brighten up the garden and add beautiful contrast to a predominantly green landscape. Hardy from Zones 4–7.

NOTABLE VARIETIES

'Candicans'. This distinct variety displays bright silvery blue needles and a distinctly upright growth habit. It looks very similar to Colorado blue spruce (*Picea pungens* var. *glauca*), only better.

Abies firma (Momi fir)

In addition to the white fir (*Abies concolor*), the Momi fir

(*A. firma*) is an excellent fir as a single specimen or in a grouping or tall screen. This species is particularly heat and drought tolerant, especially in the southeastern United States.

The dark green, stout needles and upright, conical growth habit offers a strong presence and beautiful fine texture in the landscape. The individual needles are especially unique, as the tip of the needle is clefted. The Momi fir does need room, as it can obtain heights of 40-plus ft.

Dark green needles of Momi fir

This elegant conifer prefers moist, well-drained soil and full sun but is remarkably adaptable to shade and poor soils. Hardy from Zones 6–9.

Calocedrus decurrens
California incense cedar

Since I often like to look outside the box when it comes to plants, I present to you a totally underutilized but potentially very useful conifer. The California incense cedar is a medium to slow grower, but as this West Coast native matures, it develops into quite a handsome specimen. California incense cedar looks very similar to eastern arborvitae (*Thuja occidentalis*) but is much more durable and pest resistant and becomes increasingly beautiful with age. It offers a dense, pyramidal growth habit, flats sprays of rich green leaves, and coarse, reddish brown bark. The leaves emit an aromatic odor when

Narrow, conical habit of California incense cedar

Emerald green foliage of California incense cedar

© Bruce Curtis

crushed. Although mature specimens can reach 30–50 ft. tall, they only grow about 10–15 ft. wide.

California incense cedar prefers moist, well-drained soil but adapts well to drier soil and is quite heat and drought tolerant. It thrives in full sun or partial shade but does need to be sheltered from sweeping winds.

As a screening plant, California incense cedar is an excellent choice. Although it is somewhat difficult to find in commerce, it is well worth the effort. This tree can be used in a grouping or as a single specimen and is typically most effective when placed informally in the landscape. This plant deserves more credit and attention than it gets. Hardy from Zones 5–8.

Cedrus spp.
True cedars

Arborvitae, juniper, and falsecypress are sometimes commonly referred to as red or white cedars because of their cedarlike bark and wood. However, none of these trees is a true cedar. Common names can often be misleading, but the conifers within the genus *Cedrus* are known as the true cedars. The three species of true cedars are Atlas cedar (*C. atlantica*), Deodar cedar (*C. deodara*), and cedar of Lebanon (*C. libani*). Deodar cedar is quite prevalent in the southern states, whereas Atlas cedar and cedar of Lebanon are found primarily in northern gardens.

The true cedars are all tall-growing evergreens with sharp, green needles and wide-spreading growth habits. Cedars also have large, egg-shaped female cones reaching 3–5 in. long that develop on the upper half of the tree. After two years the cones ripen and shatter, sprinkling the ground with small, brown scales.

All three of these species grow into elegant, graceful evergreens as they mature. Cedars, given proper room to grow, develop into large, upright trees over 50 ft. tall, providing an undeniable presence in the landscape. They can also function as tall screens and are especially effective in groupings or as single specimens. They are not suitable for small, residential landscapes with limited space, though. They are also not suitable as formal, pruned plantings but, rather, are appropriately used as informal plantings.

During the winter months, ice and snow collect on the strong, layered branches of cedars, making them even more noticeable in the landscape. On large sites cedars can be planted in groups of three or five with effective

Blue-green needle of blue Atlas cedar

© Bruce Curtis

Narrow, conical growth habit of fastigiate Atlas cedar

© Bruce Curtis

results. Such a grouping not only makes a bold statement but also provides an impressive, tall screen.

Cedars prefer moist, well-drained soil and full sun but adapt well to varying soils and partial shade.

Cedrus atlantica (Atlas cedar)

Atlas cedar and the popular garden variety known as blue Atlas cedar (*Cedrus atlantica* 'Glauca') become established quickly in the landscape. The plants start out as upright, strongly conical trees and eventually form a rounded, dense growth habit. The short, stout needles and long, elegant horizontal branches are particularly beautiful in the winter landscape. Atlas cedar is hardy from Zones 6–9.

NOTABLE VARIETIES

'Glauca'. The familiar blue Atlas cedar is a popular culti-vated variety with bright blue foliage.

'Fastigiata'. An excellent variety, 'Fastigiata' has an upright, narrow growth habit that is ideal for areas with limited space.

Graceful grouping of Deodar cedars in spring

© Vincent A. Simeone

Cedrus deodara (Deodar cedar)

Deodar cedar has longer, more delicate needles than the Atlas cedar (*Cedrus atlantica*). Its pyramidal, open growth habit is also quite striking. Deodar cedar is hardy from Zones 7–9.

NOTABLE VARIETY

'Kashmir'. This variety has blue-green foliage and is slightly hardier than the species.

Cedrus libani (cedar of Lebanon)

The cedar of Lebanon, the least popular of the true cedars and the most difficult to find in commerce, offers a pyramidal growth habit with horizontally layered lateral branches. Established specimens become stately over time and are most effective when used in small numbers. For example, a grouping of three will form an effective cluster and will eventually mature into a focal point in the landscape. The cedar of Lebanon has been referred to throughout antiquity. It was referred to in the Mesopotamian Epic of Gilgamesh, and many Old Testament passages use the cedar of Lebanon as a standard of beauty, grandeur, and strength. Cedar of Lebanon is hardy from Zones 5–7.

{ *Cephalotaxus harringtonia*
Japanese plum yew

Japanese plum yew is a durable evergreen shrub with narrow, lustrous, dark green leaves that are similar to those of more common yews (*Taxus* spp.; see separate entry). The leaves form a V-shaped pattern along the

© Vincent A. Simeone
Glossy foliage of plum yew

© Bruce Curtis
Plum yew in the landscape

stems and are typically not as soft to the touch as those of "true" yews. This upright, slow-growing evergreen can be maintained as a large, informal shrub or trained into more formal shapes. In either situation plum yew is a beautiful and functional needled evergreen that will offer a unique presence in the garden. Typically, it ranges in size from 5–10 ft. tall, depending on the variety.

Plum yew is a remarkably resilient shrub that prefers partial shade and moist, well-drained soil, but performs reasonably well in drier, sandy soil, heavy clay soil, and full sun or dense shade. Plum yew is generally tougher than *Taxus*, especially in the southeastern U.S., and will grow where no *Taxus* dares. This Japanese native is quite resistant to most pests and has been touted as deer resistant. It is also very adaptable to hot, dry conditions, such as areas near the seashore. Plum yew is a slow grower, needing a few years to become established in the landscape, but the patient gardener will be rewarded, since this plant improves with age. Plum yew's low-maintenance qualities and durability make it a worthwhile addition.

© Vincent A. Simeone

Cephalotaxus harringtonia 'Fastigiata' growing as an upright, dense evergreen specimen

Depending on the variety, plum yew can be used in groupings, in foundation plantings, as informal hedges, and as a screen. It is hardy from Zones 6–9, but with protection it will also grow in Zone 5. *Taxus* is typically more cold hardy, and see the separate entry on *Podocarpus macrophyllus* 'Maki' (Chinese podocarpus) for a similar plant that is adapted to even hotter climes than plum yew.

NOTABLE VARIETIES

'Duke Gardens'. Originating at Duke Gardens in North Carolina, this plum yew has a dense, spreading habit and will eventually grow to only 3 ft. tall and 4–5 ft. wide.

'Fastigiata'. It has a broad, upright growth habit up to 10 ft. tall.

'Korean Gold'. This upright shrub displays rich, golden yellow new growth before changing to green—a very nice accent in the landscape.

'Prostrata'. A useful groundcover type, growing only 2–3 ft. tall and spreading 3–4 ft. or more, 'Prostrata' makes an effective low, informal mass planting.

© Bruce Curtis

Hinoki falsecypress habit

© Bruce Curtis

Lush foliage of Hinoki falsecypress

{ *Chamaecyparis* spp.
Falsecypresses

Chamaecyparis, also known as falsecypress, is one of the most diverse and ornamental groups of all the evergreens suited for the home landscape. These trees form a pyramidal habit and provide a certain elegance that is very recognizable in the landscape. The smooth, scalelike leaves offer a soft texture in a variety of pleasing, eye-catching colors.

Chamaecyparis lawsoniana (Lawson falsecypress)

Lawson falsecypress is an elegant conifer with a pyramidal growth habit. The flat sprays of blue-green foliage are densely arranged in an upright pattern. This West Coast native can grow to a tremendous size and is not a suitable species for most residential landscape situations. There are several varieties, however, that do not get as large and can be used in smaller landscapes.

Lawson falsecypress can be effectively used in small groupings or in a formal planting as a tall screen. The tree's natural form should be maintained and no significant shearing is necessary.

Lawson falsecypress is best in colder, less humid climates and prefers rich, moist soils. It thrives in full sun or partial shade and should be kept out of excessively windy areas. Hardy from Zones 4–7.

NOTABLE VARIETIES

'Alumni'. With a columnar growth habit and blue foliage, it will grow to 25 ft.

'Columnaris'. This one has a tight columnar habit to only 15–20 ft.

'Oregon Blue'. A broad, columnar evergreen, its blue foliage is stunning.

'Pembury Blue'. This conical falsecypress with rich, blue foliage grows to 25 ft. tall.

Chamaecyparis obtusa (Hinoki falsecypress)

Hinoki falsecypress displays wavy sprays of emerald green foliage and a delightfully graceful, mounded growth habit. Mature specimens of this distinct evergreen also exhibit a flaking, reddish brown bark. Although this conifer is slow growing, it can easily grow 30 or more ft. tall and outgrow a small residential landscape. See the Notable Varieties section for dwarf varieties.

Hinoki falsecypress thrives in well-drained, rich, acidic soil and full sun or partial shade. This delicate plant should not be exposed to heavy winds, pollution, or poor, infertile soils. Pruning should be kept to a minimum, since excessive pruning will compromise its beautiful natural form.

Hinoki falsecypress is very effective along the foundation of a house, in groupings, or as a single specimen. It can also be grown in ornamental containers and urns. Hardy from Zones 5–8.

Weeping Nootka falsecypress, with its drooping lateral branches

© Bruce Curtis

NOTABLE VARIETIES

'Crippsii'. This golden variety can develop into quite a large specimen with an upright, pyramidal habit.

'Nana'. Extremely slow growing and reaching only 3–6 ft. tall, 'Nana' is ideal for a small garden.

'Nana Aurea'. This golden form remains dwarf.

'Nana Gracilis'. This variety has growth characteristics similar to those of 'Nana' but will grow taller.

Chamaecyparis nootkatensis 'Pendula' (weeping Nootka falsecypress)

Sometimes called Alaska cedar or yellow cypress, the weeping Nootka falsecypress has striking blue-green foliage and an upright yet weeping growth habit. The main trunk of this conifer grows upward, while the lateral branches hang toward the ground. This delicate, drooping habit is very picturesque, especially as the tree sways on a windy winter day.

Like most types of *Chamaecyparis*, weeping Nootka falsecypress performs best in full sun or partial shade and moist, well-drained soil. It is a stand-alone plant in the landscape and is a very effective specimen in a highly visible area of the garden. Under cultivation this evergreen typically grows 20–40 ft. tall but can get larger. Hardy from Zones 4–8.

Chamaecyparis pisifera 'Filifera' (threadleaf falsecypress)

A common evergreen, the threadleaf falsecypress displays long, threadlike, green foliage that dangles in a very graceful manner. The upright, broadly conical, semi-weeping growth habit offers a strong presence in the landscape. In groupings these conifers, also called Sawara or Japanese falsecypresses, look like large green mounds and are especially noticeable in winter. Most gardeners underestimate the ultimate size that threadleaf cypress can obtain. While these graceful conifers start slow and need time to become established, they ultimately can grow 10 to 20 or more ft. tall.

Threadleaf falsecypress prefers full sun or partial shade and moist, well-drained soil, but grows well in heavy clay and dry soils, too. Pruning can be kept to a minimum so that its naturally graceful habit is not compromised. Threadleaf falsecypress is very effective in informal groupings as a tall screen along a property boundary. Hardy from Zones 4–8.

NOTABLE VARIETIES

'Filifera Aurea'. This cultivated variety has bright golden yellow foliage. Usually 15–20 ft. tall, but I have observed mature specimens that exceeded 40 ft.

'Filifera Aurea Nana'. This truly dwarf variety is more suitable than 'Filifera Aurea' for a residential landscape. It typically grows up to 10 ft.

'Golden Mop'. This is another fine dwarf variety with a mounded habit and bright, golden yellow foliage.

Chamaecyparis thyoides (Atlantic white cedar)

The Atlantic white cedar, or white cedar falsecypress, is typically found in swampy, lowland areas of the East Coast. Commercially, this native American evergreen species is not widely available, but several exciting new varieties have emerged. Because of the improved varieties and this plant's adaptability, Atlantic white cedar has great potential as a tall screen or hedge in the landscape.

Atlantic white cedar typically grows to 40–50 ft. tall with half the spread, but the newer varieties tend to be dwarf or semi-dwarf. Some types can be used as a tall screen or windbreak, as well as—with regular shearing to keep plants contained—a tall hedge.

Atlantic white cedar prefers moist soils but will tolerate drier conditions once established. Sandy or well-drained, moist garden soils are best, but this adaptable evergreen is quite tolerant of various soil types. Full sun is best, but it tolerates partial shade, as well. Hardy from Zones 4–8 and, with some additional care in a protected location possibly 9.

NOTABLE VARIETIES

'Andelyensis'. This broadly pyramidal dwarf conifer will reach a height of only 10 ft.

'Aurea'. A conical form to 15 ft., its yellow summer foliage turns bronze in winter.

'Ericoides'. This pyramidal, compact plant has blue-green foliage that becomes purple in the winter.

'Glauca'. A pyramidal, graceful shrub, 'Glauca' has striking blue-green foliage.

'Glauca Pendula'. This unique variety has not only rich blue foliage but also drooping branches.

'Hopkinton'. Another Atlantic white cedar with blue foliage, this vigorous variety grows to 40 ft. tall.

'Red Star'. An upright, columnar plant with blue-green foliage that turns purple in the winter, it will grow 15–25 ft. tall.

'Shiva'. This variety offers a beautiful, pyramidal habit and soft, blue-green foliage.

'Variegata' ('Aureovariegata'). The foliage is marked with blotches and splashes of gold. 'Variegata' is particularly effective in partial shade.

© Bruce Curtis
Cryptomeria foliage

Cryptomeria japonica
Japanese cryptomeria

Japanese cryptomeria is an upright, dense conifer with short, medium-green, needlelike leaves spirally arranged along extended, thin stems. From winter until spring the leaves change to a bronzy color. Established specimens display a peeling, reddish brown, cedarlike bark, hence its alternate common name, Japanese cedar. Cryptomeria can grow 50 ft. or taller but typically is found in the 30–40 ft. range.

Japanese cryptomeria prefers moist, well-drained, acidic soil and full sun or partial shade. Pruning should be kept to a minimum and should be done only to remove dead twigs or leaves. Occasional pruning may be done to train this plant as a tall, dense hedge or screen.

© Vincent A. Simeone
'Yoshino' Japanese cryptomeria

Cryptomeria is an excellent specimen tree and also very useful in groupings. It can be used in the same manner as hemlock, arborvitae, and falsecypress. Hardy from Zones 5–8.

NOTABLE VARIETY

'Yoshino'. The most popular variety of Japanese cryptomeria, 'Yoshino' has rich green leaves. The beautiful green foliage color persists into the winter, although the leaves may become slightly tinged with a bronze hue.

X *Cupressocyparis leylandii*
Leyland cypress

Leyland cypress, a hybrid between a cypress (*Cupressus macrocarpa*) and Nootka falsecypress (*Chamaecyparis nootkatensis*), is a large, upright evergreen that is used extensively in the Southeast and is also becoming popular in the Northeast. Its popularity stems from its adaptability, fast growth rate, and handsome sprays of flat, dark-green or blue-green leaves. The overall growth habit is strongly pyramidal, with graceful lateral branches. Established, vigorous plants can grow up to several feet per year. Leyland cypress will grow 60–70 ft. tall and 12–20 ft. wide, although in most garden situations it is found in the 30–40 ft. height range.

Frankly, I am not enamored with Leyland cypress because it is quite overused and is susceptible to several serious pest and disease problems. There are several evergreens, such as Japanese cryptomeria (*Cryptomeria japonica*) and western arborvitae (*Thuja plicata*), that I would choose before Leyland cypress, whose worst problem is canker, a stem disease. Canker causes branch dieback to

© Vincent A. Simeone

Single specimen of Leyland cypress in the landscape

the main trunk, so it can seriously damage or kill the tree. This problem does seem to be more prevalent in the Southeast than in northern climates.

Leyland cypress prefers sun to part shade and well-drained, fertile soil. It looks best in full sun and will become thin and leggy in too much shade. Leyland cypress is very adaptable and tolerates wind, salt spray, heat, drought, and poor soil. Pruning during dry periods helps prevent disease.

Despite its disease problems and overuse, Leyland cypress could be an effective tall screen in the right landscape situation. In certain situations it may be necessary to establish evergreen cover quickly, and few plants become established as quickly in the landscape as this. (Be aware, though, that this fast-growing evergreen can rapidly outgrow its space in a small landscape.) So, Leyland cypress is a good choice for quick screens, hedges, groupings, and windbreaks, especially on a large property. Since Leyland cypress tolerates pruning, it can be trained into a formal hedge. It is most effective, however, when allowed to develop into its natural shape. Leyland cypress is very effective as a backdrop to smaller plants, but remember to give it plenty of room to grow. Hardy from Zones 6–10.

NOTABLE VARIETIES

'Castlewellan'. This striking variety with a somewhat compact habit has gold-tipped foliage, which is most pronounced in fall, winter, and spring.

'Haggerston Gray'. This variety offers irregular lateral branches and sage green foliage.

© Vincent A. Simeone

Blue foliage of Arizona cypress

'Leighton Green'. Forming a tall, columnar shape, it has dense branching and dark green foliage.

'Naylor's Blue'. This columnar form is more loosely branched and has blue-gray foliage.

'Silver Dust'. A wide-spreading form, 'Silver Dust' has blue-green foliage marked with creamy white variegation.

Cupressus arizonica
Arizona cypress

The unusual and interesting Arizona cypress has thin, blue-green foliage, interesting rounded cones, and a sturdy, upright growth habit. In addition, as specimens mature they develop rich reddish brown, flaking bark. The combination of foliage and bark in mature specimens is stunning. This conifer is fast growing and will become established quickly in a sunny area of the garden. Arizona cypress can grow over 40 ft. tall and 25 ft. wide, so it should be given ample room to grow.

Like other relatives of juniper, this species does best in full sun and well-drained soil. It is quite adaptable to a wide variety of soil types. Because of their ornamental characteristics, the cultivated varieties especially make Arizona cypress an effective accent plant or single specimen and is quite effective as a screen or windbreak. Arizona cypress also performs well near the seashore and is one of the best ornamental conifers for hot, dry, sunny conditions. Hardy from Zones 7–9.

NOTABLE VARIETIES

'Blue Ice'. This variety has beautiful silvery blue foliage that is stunning all year-round. This icy blue foliage contrasts well with the mahogany-red stems. The growth habit of 'Blue Ice' is dense and strongly conical.

Screen of 'Blue Ice' cypress

© Vincent A. Simeone

Eastern red cedar in the landscape

© Vincent A. Simeone

'Carolina Sapphire'. This is similar to 'Blue Ice' but tends to have a more open growth habit.

{ *Juniperus* spp.
Junipers

In general, junipers are overused shrubs and trees known for their adaptability and ability to tolerate harsh conditions. Junipers come in all shapes, colors, and sizes and will tolerate heat, drought, cold, pollution, and poor soil. While several common species and varieties will work as screens and hedges, such as *J. chinensis* and its cultivars, this discussion will offer just a couple that are worthy of consideration in the context of informal screens and tall hedges.

Juniperus virginiana (eastern red cedar)

Although there are dozens of species and hundreds of varieties of junipers, one fine native species, eastern red cedar (*Juniperus virginiana*), is, unfortunately, all too often overlooked. This versatile tree offers an upright conical growth habit and dark green foliage. It is widely distributed

© Vincent A. Simeone

A wall of Hollywood juniper foliage

throughout eastern and central North America and will grow just about anywhere in the landscape.

Eastern red cedar can grow into a small- or medium-sized tree, and as it matures, it develops a handsome reddish brown or gray shedding bark. The wood of this tree has a reddish pink color inside and an aromatic scent, which is where it gets its name. Often the deep green foliage turns a bronzy purple color during the winter months.

Eastern red cedar thrives in sandy, well-drained soil and full sun. However, I have observed it growing in partial shade and heavy soil. Eastern red cedar adapts to most environmental conditions, from a hot, dry, exposed seashore setting to shaded woodland. It can be used as a screening plant, in small groupings, or as a single specimen. Eastern red cedar can be pruned regularly to keep a tight habit but is much more aesthetically pleasing if left to grow naturally. Hardy from Zones 3–9.

© Vincent A. Simeone

Hollywood juniper screening a wall

Juniperus chinensis 'Torulosa' (Hollywood juniper)
Another juniper worth consideration as a screening plant is the Hollywood juniper. This juniper offers an upright, rather irregular growth habit and emerald green

foliage. It is not meant to be trained formally but is rather attractive if left to grow as an informal planting.

{ *Picea* spp.
Spruce

For many years Colorado spruce (*Picea pungens*) and the popular variety *P. pungens* var. *glauca*, with bright blue foliage, have been a conifer of choice throughout the midwestern and northeastern United States for both residential and commercial landscapes. Their cold hardiness, dense habit, and bright blue needles are a tough act to follow. Colorado spruce and a few other common species of spruce are often overused and sometimes misused, but there are several other spruces that offer enhanced aesthetic value, adaptability, and function. Given the right conditions, many species and varieties of spruce can thrive and serve various landscape functions, and some can be planted in combination with or instead of

© Bruce Curtis

Norway spruce screening a building

© Vincent A. Simeone

Colorado blue spruce sprinkled through the landscape

Colorado spruce.

Please note that the basic spruce species presented in the text may grow too large for a small landscape, so the notable garden varieties may be more appropriate for a residential site.

Picea abies (Norway spruce)

Norway spruce is a large, pyramidal conifer with long, sweeping branches and an elegant growth habit. The dark green needles and graceful, dense growth habit can add a nice backdrop to a garden in winter. This attractive evergreen can easily reach 60 or more ft. in height and must be given adequate space to grow. As the tree matures, the lower limbs arch down to the ground in a graceful manner. While Norway spruce is best suited for large, commercial sites, there are several nice dwarf forms.

Norway spruce and its varieties prefer full sun and well-drained, acidic soils with moderate moisture. The plants will tolerate partial shade and poor, rocky soil, as well. One of the most desirable attributes of Norway spruce is that, being native to Europe, it has adapted exceptionally well to North America, thriving in cool climates yet performing well in warm climates.

Norway spruce can be used as a specimen, in groupings, or as a screening plant. If the dwarf varieties are not used, careful site selection is important to ensure that the large-growing, straight species will not overwhelm your landscape. Performs best in Zones 3–7.

NOTABLE VARIETIES

'Clanbrassiliana'. This slow-growing selection forms dense mounds in the landscape and is appropriate for a home garden.

'Maxwellii'. This variety is somewhat similar to 'Clanbrassiliana' with a dwarf, mounded habit.

'Nidiformis'. The tight, spreading habit leads to this evergreen's common name, bird's nest spruce. 'Nidiformis' can be used as a foundation plant, as a companion plant to other dwarf shrubs, or in a rock garden.

'Pendula'. A peculiar-looking form, this tree has a main trunk and lateral branches that cascade toward the ground like a waterfall.

© Bruce Curtis

Graceful branching habit of Serbian spruce

Picea omorika (Serbian spruce)

Serbian spruce is an upright, narrow-growing evergreen with dark green needles that have white bands on the undersides. Often the tips of the branches are noticeably accented with a bluish white. The main trunk is particularly vertical, the lateral branches short and drooping. Mature specimens develop a distinctly vertical and graceful habit in the landscape, creating a very striking architectural outline, which is especially noticeable in winter.

Serbian spruce can grow 50 or more ft. in height but only 20 ft. wide; therefore, it can be used in a garden area where overhead space is available but there is limited width. This graceful conifer is an excellent specimen tree and can also be used effectively in small groupings. It is undoubtedly one of the most elegant conifers for the plant collector.

Serbian spruce performs best in full sun or partial shade and in moist, rich, well-drained soil. This spruce should not be planted in highly exposed, windy sites. It is an extremely adaptable and cold-hardy tree, though, thriving in Zones 4–7.

© Vincent A. Simeone

A young Oriental spruce in the landscape

© Vincent A. Simeone

Mature Oriental spruce in the landscape

NOTABLE VARIETIES

'Nana' This dwarf variety, reaching only 8–10 ft. tall, has a densely conical or rounded growth habit.

'Pendula' A very unusual-looking variety, 'Pendula' has a tall, slender main trunk and beautiful weeping side branches.

Picea orientalis (Oriental spruce)

Oriental spruce is without a doubt one of the most spectacular conifers for the garden. Few trees rival its graceful beauty. The short, glossy, dark green needles, pyramidal habit, and sweeping branches provide a four-season attraction. Oriental spruce also displays small cones, which are purple when young and eventually turn brown when mature. This elegant evergreen is a focal point in the garden, especially in winter as it glistens on a sunny day.

Although Oriental spruce does not grow quite as fast as other spruces, such as Norway (*Picea abies*) and Colorado (*P. pungens*), it is well worth the wait. I have never been disappointed with any specimen of Oriental spruce that I have encountered in the landscape.

Short needles and male cones of Oriental spruce

© Vincent A. Simeone

© Bruce Curtis

Golden yellow foliage of Oriental spruce 'Skylands'

Oriental spruce adapts well to various soils and light exposures but thrives in full sun and well-drained, moist soil. It will tolerate rocky soils but does not like arid or excessively cold environments. Like Norway spruce, this species will grow into a large specimen, so careful siting is essential, unless you get one of the cultivated varieties.

Oriental spruce is truly one of the most beautiful trees in the landscape, especially in winter. While it is spectacular all year, the winter seems to bring out the best in this wonderful landscape treasure. Oriental spruce is ideal as a single specimen or in groupings. On my top ten list of favorite trees, this is ranked very high, at number 2. Hardy from Zones 4–7.

NOTABLE VARIETIES

'Gowdy'. A compact variety with a dense, narrow habit, it reaches only 8–10 ft.

'Gracilis'. A beautiful selection with a dense, conical growth habit to 15–20 ft. tall.

'Nana'. This globular, low-growing variety matures at only a few feet tall and wide.

'Skylands'. Here's an interesting form whose bright golden yellow needles will add a nice splash of color to a green landscape.

{ *Pinus* spp.
Pines

Pines are a very diverse and widely used group of trees that are prominent fixtures in the winter landscape. The soft, fine texture of the needles and the interesting bark and growth habit are three important ornamental characteristics. While there are many to choose from, here are a few choice species worth serious consideration.

Pinus bungeana (lacebark pine)

The lacebark pine is truly one of the most carefree and beautiful conifers available. It has an interesting upright growth habit and dark, thick, glossy green needles. But the most interesting attribute of this plant is the multicolored, exfoliating bark, which displays shades of green, tan, brown, and white.

An established lacebark pine can be effective as a single specimen or in a small grouping. Mature specimens reach 30–50 ft. tall and 20–30 ft. wide. This choice species is tolerant of drought, pests, and various soil types. Although it prefers sun, lacebark pine is very adaptable to shade. Lacebark pine is hardy from Zones 4–7, but it should be sited in a sheltered location in Zone 4.

© Vincent A. Simeone

Lacebark pine with silvery gray bark in the landscape

© Vincent A. Simeone

Dense, rounded habit of lacebark pine

Blue-green foliage of Korean pine

© Vincent A. Simeone

Pinus koraiensis (Korean pine)

Korean pine, a close relative of the widespread eastern white pine (*Pinus strobus*), can add great interest to the winter landscape. Korean pine has dense, stout tufts of growth that have a distinct bluish green color. This striking color is especially noticeable in the midst of a freshly fallen snow.

Pinus parviflora (Japanese white pine)

Japanese white pine is an irregularly growing, semi-dwarf pine with blue-green foliage. The short, soft, blue-green needles and picturesque character of the habit are very handsome. It is a wonderful specimen tree for a woodland setting among rhododendrons and other broadleaf evergreens. Japanese white pine can also be featured in a lawn area in full sun.

Mature specimens can range from 25–50 ft. tall, with a similar spread. Hardy from Zones 4–7.

Upright habit of the 'Fastigiata' white pine

© Vincent A. Simeone

Pinus strobus
(eastern white pine)

Eastern white pine, also known simply as white pine, grows from Canada to the southeastern and midwestern United States and is one of the most popular native pines.

White pine grouping in the landscape

Its flexible, blue-green foliage is very soft to the touch. The species develops into a large, magnificent tree, but too large for the average garden—mature specimens grow 60 ft. and greater. However, several eastern white pine varieties are appropriate for the home landscape.

Eastern white pine grows best in deep, rich, acidic soil and full sun or partial shade. It needs adequate moisture and protection from harsh winds. This soft-wooded tree is often damaged by high winds and heavy snow and ice accumulations. Hardy from Zones 3–8.

NOTABLE VARIETIES

'Compacta'. Popularly known as dwarf eastern white pine, this is a slow-growing, dense form that will eventually reach 8–10 ft. tall, with an equal spread. It can be used as a single specimen or in groupings strategically placed in the landscape.

'Fastigiata'. This is one of the best varieties of white pine to use as a tall screen. It has a dense, strongly upright, narrow growth habit and tends not to spread as wide as the species, making it more suitable for an area where space is limited.

'Pendula'. A very interesting selection, 'Pendula' has a main trunk and side branches that weep toward the ground, creating a flowing appearance with age. It is typically used as a single specimen that can be viewed from all sides.

Pinus wallichiana (Himalayan pine)

Like Korean pine (*Pinus koraiensis*), a close relative of the eastern white pine (*P. strobus*), the Himalayan pine (*P. wallichiana*) can brighten up the winter scene. Sometimes called Bhutan pine after the Himalayan kingdom, it has beautiful semi-pendulous branches and long, drooping needles. The graceful growth habit and blue-green, softly textured needles make this a showpiece in the landscape.

NOTABLE VARIETY

'Zebrina' This striking variegated selection of Himalayan pine has yellow-striped foliage.

{ *Podocarpus macrophyllus* 'Maki'
Chinese podocarpus

A narrow-leaved evergreen species to consider, especially in the warmer southern climates of the United States, is Chinese podocarpus (*Podocarpus macrophyllus* 'Maki'). Podocarpus has leaves similar to, but noticeably larger than, those of the common yews (*Taxus* spp.) and the Japanese plum yew (*Cephalotaxus harringtonia*). This adaptable shrub or small tree can tolerate shearing or regular pruning, various soil types, shade, heat, drought, and even deer. It is primarily found in Zones 8–10.

Chinese podocarpus, also called the shrubby or 'Maki' podocarpus, is ideal as a formal or informal hedge or tall screen. It can be shaped or utilized in various landscape situations. Podocarpus prefers moist, well drained soil and full sun or partial shade but is very adaptable. It can reach 20 or more ft. in height, but it can be kept substantially smaller with proper pruning.

NOTABLE VARIETIES

'Brodie'. This is a shrubby, dense form growing 3 ft. tall by 6 ft. wide.

Formal tall hedge of *Podocarpus*

Podocarpus foliage

© Vincent A. Simeone

'Nana'. A bushy variety, it has a rounded, spreading habit.

{ *Pseudotsuga menzesii*
Douglasfir

Douglasfir is a popular conifer native to the western United States. While it performs best in cooler climates and mountainous areas, it has emerged as landscape plant for various uses and applications. Douglasfir performs best in the colder climates, Zone 3–6, but it will also tolerate the northern areas of Zone 7. Unfortunately, in warmer, humid climates this tree is not particularly vigorous or effective.

One of the main reasons Douglasfir is so popular is that it grows rather quickly when young and forms a tight, dense, pyramidal form. The soft, grayish green needles offer a fine texture in the landscape. Ultimately, this conifer can grow 40–80 ft. tall in cultivation, so it is best used at larger, commercial sites, such as college campuses, golf courses, and parks.

Douglasfir prefers rich, moist, well drained soil and full sun or partial shade. It also prefers to be sheltered from high winds or an unusual degree of exposure. If sited properly, this popular evergreen can be used in groupings or as a single specimen, either of which will function as a tall screen.

{ *Sciadopitys verticillata*
Japanese umbrella pine

Japanese umbrella pine, or simply umbrella pine, is a unique and beautiful conifer that will undoubtedly stand out in the landscape. The slender, dark green leaves radiate around the end of the stems in a circular pattern, creating an umbrella-like appearance. The strong, pyramidal growth habit, dense branching, and shedding, reddish brown bark are also admirable ornamental qualities. Foliage usually hides the bark unless the tree's lower limbs are removed, though.

Once established, Japanese umbrella pine develops a distinctive and very handsome appearance. Mature specimens can easily grow to 30 ft., but umbrella pine is a slow-growing tree. It

© Bruce Curtis

Umbrella pine in winter

© Bruce Curtis

Thick, glossy needles of umbrella pine

prefers full sun or partial shade and moist, well-drained, acidic soils. Pruning should be kept to a minimum and is usually necessary only if a broken or damaged branch is in need of attention.

Japanese umbrella pine is ideal as a single specimen in an open lawn area. It is especially noticeable in the winter, when it stands out against the bare landscape. Hardy from Zones 5–7.

NOTABLE VARIETIES

'Aurea'. This golden form has striking yellow foliage that provides an attractive accent to the landscape.

'Jim Cross'. This variety is named after the late, great nurseryman from Environmentals Nursery on Long Island, New York.

'Ossorio Gold'. Here's another golden type somewhat similar to 'Aurea'.

{ *Sequoiadendron giganteum*
Sierra redwood

This elegant West Coast native should not be confused with the true giant redwoods of the coast (Sequoia sempervirens). Although *Sequoiadendron* also matures to a stately tree, it is much

Conical growth habit of young Sierra redwood

Blue-green foliage of Sierra redwood

more suitable for the climate of the northeastern and southeastern United States. Sierra redwood can reach enormous heights in its native habitat, but out east it tends to be a bit more subdued. Typically, this slow grower is found in the landscape as a dense, conical tree reaching 40–50 ft. In ideal situations in the Pacific Northwest of North America, Sierra redwood can get considerably larger, and for this reason it is best in a larger commercial site. The fine, blue-green, pointed leaves and spongy, reddish brown bark are attractive features in the landscape. As young trees, they are tightly pyramidal and dense, and they mature to great majesty and beauty.

This drought-tolerant, pest-resistant tree prefers most, well drained soil and full sun or partial shade. It can be used effectively in groupings, in mass plantings, as a single specimen, or as a tall, informal screen. Hardy from Zones 6–8.

NOTABLE VARIETY
'Hazel Smith'. This variety has striking blue foliage and improved cold hardiness.

{ *Taxus* spp.
Yew

Somewhat overused evergreens, yews can function as effective hedges and screens, but there are several important factors that must be considered before planting. First and foremost, yews need well-drained soil. Poorly drained, heavy soil often results in plants declining and succumbing to root rot. For best results moist, well-drained soil and full sun or partial shade are best. Yews are very prone to deer browsing and damage from such insect pests as scale, weevil, and mealybug.

Yews offer dark, finely textured, needlelike foliage; red, fleshy covered seeds (not edible); and reddish brown bark that peels with age. The stunning bark is more obvious on established specimens that are of considerable size. The broad, spreading or upright habit and densely arranged branches produce a rather strong presence in the landscape. Yews are highly tolerant of regular shearing and pruning and can even be severely pruned, if necessary, when dormant in late winter.

The three species of yews that are most available in commerce are English yew (*Taxus baccata*), Japanese yew (*T. cuspidata*), and *Taxus* × *media*, an intermediate hybrid between the two. Yew is highly cultivated, with dozens of varieties available, offering many shapes and sizes. For somewhat similar alternatives to *Taxus* that can take more southern heat, see the separate entries on *Cephalotaxus harringtonia* (Japanese plum yew) and *Podocarpus macrophyllus* 'Maki' (Chinese podocarpus).

© Vincent A. Simeone

Taxus × *media* in the winter landscape

Yews are very popular evergreens that have a variety of landscape applications, including formal and informal hedges, screens, and foundation plantings. Very often yews are found pruned unmercifully to create tight boxes, rounded gumdrop shapes, or any number of other unnatural forms. But if left unpruned, yews can mature into wonderful, wide-spreading specimen trees.

My conclusion about using yews as hedges and screens is simple: They work in certain situations, but there are many other worthy shrubs that should be considered first. If specifically yew-friendly landscape siting (good drainage, light, and so on) and culture can be provided, though, then go for it.

English spreading yew in the landscape

Taxus baccata (English yew)

English yew is also known as the common yew. It is hardy from Zones 5–7. Its adaptability and exceptionally dark green foliage make this shrub or small tree a real standout in the landscape. Mature specimens of English yew display a striking reddish brown bark that peels off from the trunk in sheets. The garden varieties listed below are among the best and are available in the horticultural trade.

NOTABLE VARIETIES

'Fastigiata'. This variety has a columnar shape, and mature specimens grow 20–30 ft. tall but only 4–8 ft. wide.

'Repandens'. A popular, elegant variety of English yew, 'Repandens' is a low, mounded form with cascading branches, in contrast to 'Fastigiata'. Mature specimens typically reach 2–4 ft. tall and twice as wide. This form has a very distinct, semi-weeping habit.

Taxus cuspidata (Japanese yew)

Japanese yew can take a bit more cold than English yew, and is hardy to Zone 4. Japanese yew offers short, medium to dark green leaves, and a dense, upright habit. Like English yew, Japanese yew also displays rich, reddish brown, exfoliating bark with age. Often garden varieties are selected rather than the straight species.

NOTABLE VARIETY

'Capitata'. Also known as the "Cap" yew, this strongly vertical grower is often pruned formally into tight, pyramidal shapes.

'Nana'. A popular variety of the Japanese yew, 'Nana' is relatively slow growing, with a spreading, dense habit. It eventually reaches 10-plus ft. high, with double the spread.

Taxus × media

Taxus × media is a cross between English yew (*T. baccata*) and Japanese yew (*T. cuspidata*). Like the latter, this hybrid is hardy to Zone 4. This hybrid yew is by far the most popular species available in commerce. Although not used as widely as it once was, *Taxus × media* is still used as hedges and screens in northern climates. *Taxus × media* has a dense, shrubby, upright, and spreading habit, but, unlike the former two species mentioned, is not known for its ornamental bark characteristics.

NOTABLE VARIETY

'Hicksii'. One could spend a lifetime researching the various varieties of *Taxus* × *media*, but 'Hicksii' is by far the most widely used. The Hicks yew is most often used for formal and informal hedges.

{ *Thuja* spp.
Arborvitae

Arborvitae, Latin for "tree of life," is a popular landscape evergreen that has been an integral part of the American landscape for decades. American arborvitae (*Thuja occidentalis*) is a very common and in fact overused evergreen found in many commercial and residential landscapes across the United States. Western arborvitae (*T. plicata*), a lesser-known species, is a superior alternative. For another evergreen that looks a lot like arborvitae but is stronger and more problem free, see the entry on California incense cedar (*Calocedrus decurrens*).

© Bruce Curtis

American arborvitae as a screen

Western arborvitae's graceful habit after a freshly fallen snow

Mature single specimen of western arborvitae

Thuja occidentalis (American arborvitae)

American arborvitae does offer garden merit but is typically shorter lived than western arborvitae and just not nearly as durable. American arborvitae, also known as eastern arborvitae and white cedar, can be quite susceptible to breakage from high winds and heavy snow, which is not an issue with western arborvitae. Fortunately, there are several improved varieties of American arborvitae to choose from.

NOTABLE VARIETY

'Emerald'. This variety, also known as 'Smaragd', is the most popular, with deep emerald green foliage and a tight, conical growth habit.

Thuja plicata (western arborvitae)

A beautiful evergreen, western arborvitae has a graceful pyramidal growth habit and smooth, emerald green leaves that look good year-round. Western arborvitae has fewer problems and tends to age much more gracefully than its East Coast counterpart, American arborvitae. It is also a superb replacement for such native species as Canadian hemlock that have been

'Atrovirens' foliage

© Vincent A. Simeone

decimated by pest problems in the northeastern United States. It makes a much better landscape tree than, for example, Leyland cypress, an overused and fast-growing evergreen.

Upon a recent visit to the Canadian Rockies and Vancouver, I was in awe of the towering specimens of western arborvitae in the mountainous forests. The semi-pendulous branches and bright green, ferny new growth was nothing short of spectacular.

Western arborvitae is extremely adaptable, tolerating poor soil, varying soil pH, wind, drought, and other adverse conditions. During the winter months, it is quite durable, handling weighty snow loads and desiccating winds that would damage other trees. It is also very tolerant of light exposure and in fact thrives in full sun, but it is also very shade tolerant. It does best in moist, well-drained soil. Hardy from Zones 4–8.

Western arborvitae, also known as giant arborvitae and western red cedar, can grow quite large—50 ft. tall and 30 ft. wide at maturity—and must be sited in an area of the garden where it can grow freely. Western arborvitae can be kept "under control," however, with regular judicious pruning. It is excellent as a single specimen or can be used in a grouping to create an impenetrable screen. There are several excellent garden varieties that are wonderful additions to the landscape.

Western arborvitae is an absolute knockout that has my vote as number 1 screening plant of all the conifers. It is truly one of the best evergreens for tall screens where space is available. In addition to being a great landscape plant, western arborvitae is valued for its wood and has been used for making shingles, fence posts, greenhouse framing, and other structures. It is also touted as deer resistant.

NOTABLE VARIETIES

'Atrovirens'. A common variety with deep green foliage and an open pyramidal habit, this can be used as a single specimen or as a tall screen. As it matures, it creates an impenetrable mass of foliage.

'Green Giant'. This hybrid arborvitae has gained in popularity in recent years. It offers a rich, medium to dark green foliage, and a tight, narrow, pyramidal growth habit.

'Virescens'. Another choice variety, 'Virescens' has a tight, conical habit and dark green foliage. It is suitable for a garden area with limited space.

Broadleaf Evergreens

An evergreen is defined as a plant that retains its leaves throughout the year. Evergreens add distinct beauty and structure to the landscape. In general terms, evergreens are classified as either broadleaf or narrow-leaved. Narrow-leaved evergreens—also referred to as needled evergreens—have thin, needlelike foliage, as is the case, for example, with pines and spruces. Evergreen plants that have wide leaves, such as hollies and rhododendrons, are known as broadleaf evergreens.

The term *evergreen* is relative, given the fact that all evergreens eventually lose all of their leaves—just not all at once. Most evergreens retain their foliage for several years, with the older foliage being replaced by new foliage. For example, during the fall the older needles of pine trees drop, littering the ground, while the newest growth is retained.

The broadleaf evergreens discussed in this book give gardeners excellent choices for enhancing the garden. These plants provide rich foliage color and pleasing textures that present a beautiful backdrop or a focal point in the landscape. In addition to superior foliage, many broadleaf evergreens also display beautiful flowers and fruit. Whether used as a single specimen or in groupings, an evergreen is an integral part of the garden and is most apparent during winter. Most importantly, because broadleaf evergreens have large, lush leaves, they make excellent screening plants.

Aucuba japonica 'Variegata'
Gold dust plant

The beautiful gold dust plant is a good example of the bold texture that a broadleaf evergreen can add to the landscape. This cultivated shrub offers dark, lustrous, green leaves with speckles, splashes, and blotches of gold or yellow that provide year-round interest in the garden, as do the *Aucuba japonica* varieties 'Picturata' and 'Sulphur'. Gold dust plant also has interesting thick, smooth, green stems. Gold dust plant can reach 6–10 ft. in height, with slightly less of a spread, and mature plantings can create a dense wall of growth.

Aucuba prefers partial shade and well-drained, moist soil with ample amounts of organic matter. It will tolerate dense shade, but beware of placing it in full sun, which will result in a bleaching or scalding of the leaves. Pruning can be kept to a minimum, but occasional selective pruning to remove weak old stems is advisable. Stems can also be harvested and used for decorations during the holidays. While gold dust plant can be pruned formally as a tight hedge, it is much more effective as an informal planting.

© Bruce Curtis

Mass planting of gold dust plant

© Bruce Curtis

Speckled foliage of gold dust plant

Gold dust plant makes a bold statement in the landscape and is suitable in groupings and mass plantings. It can make a very effective screen in a shade garden. It is also very effective as an accent plant because of its variegated leaves. Gold dust plant is hardy from Zones 7–10, but it will grow in Zone 6 in a protected location.

{ *Berberis julianae*
Wintergreen barberry

An upright, mounded evergreen, wintergreen barberry has thick, glossy, green leaves that change to bronzy red during the cold winter months. Wintergreen barberry is a vigorous grower that forms a dense, rounded mass of growth reaching 6–8 ft. or more in height. In early spring, bright golden yellow flower clusters develop along each stem. These attributes make wintergreen barberry a four-season plant.

Wintergreen barberry is an extremely resilient shrub, tolerating most soil types, provided they are well drained. They tolerate shade but thrive in full sun. For best results this evergreen barberry should be planted in moist, acidic, well-drained soil. Wintergreen barberry is remarkably tolerant of heat, drought, cold, and sandy or heavy clay soil. It's also very tolerant of seashore conditions of salt spray and wind.

Since barberry has sharp thorns several inches long, siting should be carefully considered when planting this shrub. You don't want it to be a threat to draw blood while your family and you are trying to relax and enjoy the yard. However, few shrubs will be as effective as a barrier hedge or screen.

Wintergreen barberry is also effective in mass plantings or groupings. Because it is tolerant of pruning, wintergreen barberry can be trained as a formal hedge or as an informal hedge, depending on the intended purpose. 'William Penn', a hybrid barberry with similar features to wintergreen barberry, is a popular garden variety with a semi-dwarf growth habit. Hardy from Zones 5–8.

© Vincent A. Simeone

Hedge of common boxwood

© Vincent A. Simeone

Boxwood and yew in a formal English garden

{ *Buxus* spp.
Boxwoods

Many of the plants in this book are a bit of a divergence from the norm, but there are some old favorites we come back to. For centuries one of the most popular and signature evergreens for hedges and foundation plantings has been boxwood (*Buxus* spp.). Today mainstream plants like boxwood are often overlooked because of the draw of more exciting species of evergreens emerging onto the market. However, boxwood can still be found in many landscape applications, from formal hedges to informal mass plantings to topiary (sculpting into desired shapes, such as geometric or animal figures).

Unfortunately, boxwood is a rather finicky plant, requiring good drainage and fertile soil as well as adequate moisture. In addition, several serious insect pests and diseases make boxwood somewhat of a high-maintenance liability in a residential landscape. Often horticulturists recommend Japanese holly (*Ilex crenata*) as a substitute because it is much more durable.

Although boxwood is not typically considered an ideal evergreen for the home garden, I'd like to mention a few selections that are worthy of landscape use.

Buxus sempervirens
(common boxwood, common box)

Common boxwood may be the most widespread species of boxwood and if it is given the right environmental conditions and used correctly, it is quite elegant. With pruning, this plant can be maintained anywhere from a few feet to 5 or 6 ft. high. This species is hardy from Zones 5–8, depending on the variety.

NOTABLE VARIETY

'Suffruticosa'. This is the most popular type of common boxwood. A compact form, it is often used as an edging plant. 'Suffruticosa' is often pruned formally into tight, manicured hedges or to define formal edges.

OTHER *BUXUS* VARIETIES

Types of littleleaf boxwood (*Buxus microphylla*) or hybrids of various species have emerged as good garden plants. Some of the best include 'Green Gem', 'Green Mound', 'Green Velvet', 'Winter Gem', and 'Wintergreen'. All are valued for their compact growth habit, rich green color, and cold hardiness. Hardy from Zones 5–8.

Camellia spp.
Camellias

Camellias are garden favorites and have long been admired as among the most exotic and showy evergreen flowering shrubs. In the eighteenth century, camellias were imported to Europe and America from Japan and China, where they grow in the mountains. For many years they were thought to be tender and considered only for greenhouse collections, especially in colder climates. But in several parts of the United States, such as the Southeast and the West Coast, camellias grow outdoors.

Camellias are excellent screening plants because of their large, thick, glossy leaves and upright, dense growth habit. Camellias can be grown as shrubs or even trees reaching 10 ft. or taller. There are two main species valued as garden ornamentals in America, Japanese camellia (*Camellia japonica*) and sasanqua camellia (*C. sasanqua*). These ornamental camellias are close relatives of the tea plant (*C. sinensis*), which is of course a major economic crop.

While the main priority of this book is to expound the virtues of evergreens' landscape functions, camellias also have much to offer gardeners ornamentally. Camellia flowers are quite diverse, with many different flower colors and types available. Flowers range from white to pink to red as well as two-tone flowers. Camellia flower types can also vary from single to semi-double or double and can mimic other flowers, such as peonies and anemones. Camellia foliage is quite striking as it matures to a lustrous, dark green. As the plants mature, the thin, smooth, tan or gray bark is also rather handsome.

Although adaptable, camellias have specific cultural needs that should be followed in order for them to perform to their maximum potential. They thrive in moist, well-drained, acidic soil rich in organic material. Camellias prefer light, dappled shade and mulch, which will help protect their shallow root systems. Mulch can consist of shredded leaves or compost. Several pests, including scale and spider mites, can provide a challenge to the gardener growing camellias, so they should be closely monitored. If a pest problem occurs, take a sample to your local agricultural extension service for evaluation and suggested treatment.

Camellias in flower

Dense habit of camellia

Pruning to shape plants or maintain dense habits can be done after flowering. All too often camellia plants are pruned regularly to form a dense, formal hedge or screen, but maintaining them as informal plantings will produce more flowers and an overall healthier plant. If severe pruning is needed, wait until late winter or early spring, when the shrubs are dormant. This type of pruning will reduce flowering the first year but will stimulate the plant to produce a healthy crop of flowers the following years. Camellias can reach 8–12 ft. in height and 6–10 ft. wide but can be kept smaller with judicious pruning. Although camellias thrive in moist, cool environments, they are remarkably tolerant of hot, humid conditions, provided they receive adequate, regular watering.

Camellias are excellent flowering shrubs and small trees for adding structure and beauty to the landscape. Their long-lasting blooming period, upright growth habit, and lustrous, bold foliage offer great texture and color to the garden. Camellias can be used in groupings and shade gardens and can also be grown as informal hedges, screens, or as individual specimens.

While camellias have traditionally been considered landscape favorites for warmer, moderate climates, extensive research has produced many cold-hardy new varieties that can be used in colder climates, as well. The majority of these cold-hardy selections are the result of extensive work done by two scientists, Dr. Ackerman and Dr. Parks. The Ackerman hybrids are primarily hybrids of several different species, while the Parks types are hybrids and choice selections of Japanese camellia.

Camellias flower in either fall or spring, depending on the species and variety chosen. In any case, camellias used in colder climates outdoors should be sited carefully, not in cold, windy, and exposed areas of the garden. If used as a screen, a shady, somewhat protected location in the garden is preferred. In fact, like rhododendrons and viburnums, camellias are very good screening plants for shade.

One key element in successfully growing camellias is the time of year they are planted. Timing of planting depends on the climate you are growing them in. To ensure success, camellia plants should be planted when weather conditions are mild and optimum for root growth in your garden. In the North camellias should be planted in spring, after the harsh, cold winter temperatures have subsided. The plants will develop root and top growth during the spring and summer, before the onset of the cooler temperatures of autumn. Of course, regular watering in times of summer drought is also very important. In addition, camellias planted in colder climates should be given northern or western exposure to avoid morning sun in winter. If sited incorrectly, camellias would be more susceptible to winter damage and leaf desiccation.

© Vincent A. Simeone

Flowering hardy camellia in the landscape

In gardens in the South, on the other hand, fall planting is recommended, after the harsh heat of the summer has passed. In the South the soil temperatures in fall and early winter tend to be optimal for root growth, since freezing occurs less often and is less severe than in northern climates. Camellias planted in the fall in southern gardens will establish roots during the cooler season, before the heat of summer approaches the following growing season.

Although there are many fine hardy camellia selections available, let's discuss a few of the most garden-worthy varieties. Many more good performers can be sought in nursery catalogs and on the worldwide web.

Camellia japonica (Japanese camellia)

Japanese camellia varieties typically flower from early

to late spring. The Japanese camellia selections and hybrids discussed below are most reliable in Zones 7–9, although they will also grow fine in Zone 6 if properly sited in a protected location.

NOTABLE VARIETIES

'April Blush'. This variety grows into a bushy plant with deep green leaves and shell pink, semi-double blooms.

'April Rose'. This compact and rather slow-growing plant has rose red double flowers. It is very floriferous and will bloom in midspring.

'April Snow'. This relatively slow-growing plant has white, rose-form double flowers. It provides a profuse display of color in mid to late spring.

'Korean Fire'. A proven performer, this is one of the most cold-hardy varieties of camellia. 'Korean Fire' blooms heavily, with single red flowers with bright yellow centers, in early to midspring.

'Kumasaka'. One of the oldest varieties of camellia, this has been grown in Japan since 1695. The double blooms are red or deep rose and open late in spring.

'Lady Clare'. This variety has semi-double pink flowers.

Camellia hybrids

The Ackerman hybrids are primarily hybrids of several different species. Hybrids with *Camellia sasanqua* influence bloom in mid to late fall, while *C. japonica* hybrids bloom in spring.

© Bruce Curtis

Hardy *Camellia* 'Mason Farm' in bloom

NOTABLE VARIETIES

'Mason Farm'. This vigorous grower offers large white flowers tinged with pink and is a fall bloomer. The thick, leathery leaves are quite handsome against the pure white blooms.

'Pink Icicle'. This hybrid from Dr. Ackerman has shell pink, peony-form flowers in early spring.

'Polar Ice'. The white double flowers open in the mid fall on upright branches. The plant will grow to 6 ft. by 6 ft. in ten years.

'Snow Flurry'. This vigorous plant produces masses of flowers each year. Its nearly pure-white flowers often make this one of the first camellias to open in the fall. Young plants often have a spreading habit, so some pruning may be needed.

'Winter's Charm'. The striking lavender-pink flowers are semi-double and open in mid to late fall.

'Winter's Hope'. This early-blooming cultivar has white flowers and a dense, spreading growth habit.

'Winter's Interlude'. The bicolor flower offers pink outer petals and many small white petals in the center. The spreading growth matures into a rounded shrub with deep, glossy green leaves.

'Winter's Rose'. This dwarf camellia grows 3 ft. wide and 3–4 ft. tall. Pale pink double flowers are produced in profusion in mid to late fall.

'Winter's Star'. Single flowers are a reddish purple and emerge in mid to late fall.

Camellia sasanqua (sasanqua camellia)

Along with Japanese camellia (*Camellia japonica*) and its hybrids, sasanqua camellia is an exceptional, fall-blooming evergreen shrub. It displays white, pink, or red flowers. *Camellia sasanqua* and its hybrids bloom in mid to late fall.

This species is generally smaller than Japanese camellia, growing 6–10 ft. tall. The plant also has a finer texture than Japanese camellia but is still equally effective as a screen or a hedge. It is fast growing and will usually develop into a dense shrub within a few growing seasons. It is hardy from Zones 7–9 but should be protected in northern gardens.

NOTABLE VARIETY

'Cleopatra'. This is a vigorous grower with pink, semi-double flowers and an upright habit.

Euonymus kiautschovicus
Spreading euonymus

Spreading euonymus is a fast-growing evergreen shrub with rich, dark green, glossy leaves. It can be semi-evergreen in the harsh, cold winters of the northeastern and midwestern states. Although many species of *Euonymus* are overused and can become troublesome in the garden, this species is rather useful. It is a rounded shrub reaching 8–10 ft. tall and wide. The small, greenish white flowers appear in late summer, and bees are attracted to them, so careful siting away from areas where people congregate is important. In late fall the pinkish fruit capsules appear, opening up to expose the orange seeds.

Spreading euonymus thrives in full sun or partial shade and moist, well-drained soil, but those conditions are not necessary for this plant to succeed. It is very adaptable and will tolerate poor soil, pollution, and excessive shade. This shrub also takes regular pruning quite well, which is why it is an excellent choice as a hedge or a screen.

Because of the flowers, spreading euonymus is not a good selection near a patio or outdoor seating area. It is, however, good for mass planting, informal or formal hedges, and screens. It is not as susceptible to scale and other common problems associated with other members of the genus, such as winter creeper euonymus (*Euonymus fortunei*) and Japanese euonymus (*E. japonicus*).

NOTABLE VARIETY

'Manhattan'. This is the most popular variety of spreading euonymus. It is particularly vigorous and cold hardy—from Zones 5–8.

Glossy foliage and greenish white flowers of spreading euonymus

Spreading, informal growth habit of euonymus

{ *Ilex* spp.
Hollies

Hollies are among the most useful and popular of all broadleaf evergreen trees and shrubs. While hollies tend to blend into the landscape most of the year, in late autumn, as the berries ripen and deciduous trees shed their leaves, these bold evergreens come to life with landscape interest. Evergreen hollies are grown for their beautiful foliage, showy fruit, and dense growth habit. In general, hollies are easy-to-grow, adaptable landscape plants that tolerate pruning and varying soil types, soil pH levels, and degrees of light exposure. Because of their dense habit, adaptability, and ornamental qualities, hollies are very useful screening plants.

One very important fact about hollies is that they are dioecious, meaning male and female flowers are borne on separate plants. Therefore, female plants need separate male pollen producers nearby in order to bear fruit. One male plant can pollinate many female plants; however, like species should be used for pollination. For example, an American holly (*Ilex opaca*) female should receive pollen from an American holly male, not from the male of another species, such as English holly (*I. aquifolium*).

Though the priority when planting hollies is usually to provide a thick screen, the fruit does add interest in the winter months. It is important to note that while hollies are very tolerant of pruning, timing is everything. As a general rule, if severe (more than 50%) pruning is needed, the best time to perform this is late winter or early spring. If your hollies are the right size and only maintenance pruning or shearing is needed to maintain a formal hedge, that pruning can be done during the growing season, preferably after the plants have flowered. If pruning is done after flowering, though, less fruit will be available in the fall.

Ilex aquifolium (English holly)

English holly has beautiful glossy foliage that glistens in the sun during the winter. The spiny, dark green leaves have a lustrous finish that is quite handsome all year. During the fall large, juicy, red fruits ripen; they usually persist most of the winter, until birds eat them. The tall, pyramidal growth habit and horizontal side branches provide structure in the landscape. There are many cultivated varieties of English holly available, with selections offering red or yellow berries, variegated foliage, and various growth patterns.

English holly prefers moist, well-drained, acidic soil and full sun or partial shade. It does not do particularly well in windy, exposed sites. It can even suffer from leaf burn during the winter, caused by a combination of cold temperatures and strong, drying winds. In most cases the damaged leaves will fall off in the spring and be replaced with new leaves.

This species can grow over 20 ft. tall, so adequate room is needed to accommodate its robust size. English holly will tolerate regular pruning to maintain a dense habit or severe pruning to rejuvenate overgrown plants. Maintenance, or light, pruning can be performed in summer, whereas severe pruning should be done in late winter or early spring.

English holly can be grown as a single specimen, in groupings, as a screening plant, or as a hedge. It can be pruned as a formal hedge but is much more effective as an informal hedge or tall screen. Regular formal pruning will reduce fruit set. The cut branches are highly valued during the holiday season for arrangements and holiday displays. Hardy from Zones 6–7.

Ilex cornuta 'Burfordii' (Burford holly)

Several species of holly are more adaptable than most to the hot, humid summers of the southern United States. Burford holly, a form of Chinese holly (the *Ilex cornuta* species), is exceptionally tolerant of hot, humid climates with periods of drought, making it a better choice than Japanese holly (*I. crenata*) in the South. Burford holly has dark green, lustrous leaves with a rich, glossy sheen. The berries ripen to a reddish orange in fall and persist into the winter.

Burford holly is extensively used in the South for formal and informal hedges and low screens. The plants have a dwarf, dense growth habit, generally reaching 3–4 ft. tall, with a similar spread. Hardy from Zones 7–10.

Ilex crenata (Japanese holly)

Japanese holly is one of the best evergreen hollies for screens and hedges. Its dense habit and adaptability make it very versatile in the landscape. Japanese holly has small, rounded leaves and a rounded or upright growth habit. In fall it develops small, black fruits, which are rather inconspicuous. Japanese holly can reach 5–10 ft. tall, with an equal spread. In shade mature plants become more open, whereas in sun plants develop thick, dense masses of growth.

Japanese holly pruned formally

Japanese holly hedge pruned informally

Japanese holly prefers moist, well-drained soil and full sun or partial shade, but it is remarkably shade tolerant. It is extremely forgiving of pruning and can be trained into hedges and screens rather easily. Japanese holly will grow in a wide variety of soil types and pH levels. Hardy from Zones 5–8, Japanese holly tends to perform better in colder climates.

This shrub typically has a medium growth rate and can be used in a variety of ways. If left unpruned, Japanese holly will form a mounded, dense habit and will function as a screen or an informal hedge. It can also be pruned regularly to create a formal, sheared hedge, which allows the gardener to create a more formal, controlled look.

NOTABLE VARIETIES

There are many cultivars of Japanese holly, ranging from miniatures to larger types. For the purpose of this book, here are a few common varieties that can serve as living screens or informal and formal hedges.

'Compacta'. With a dense, semi-dwarf habit, this is ideal as a formal hedge or screen.

'Convexa'. This vigorous grower has shiny, convex leaves and a spreading, rounded habit, 6–8 ft. tall and wide.

'Helleri'. A dense, mounded shrub that looks like a giant mushroom as it matures, this variety is suitable as a low screen or informal hedge.

'Hetzii'. It is similar to 'Convexa' but with larger leaves and larger female fruit. Grows 6–8 ft. tall and wide.

'Jersey Pinnacle'. A beautiful introduction from Dr. Elwin Orton of Rutgers University, it has a dense, compact, upright growth habit to 6 ft. tall and 4 ft. wide, with dark green, glossy foliage.

'Sky Pencil'. An introduction through the Elite Plant Program of the U.S. National Arboretum, this fastigiate grower can reach 10 ft. tall and only 2–3 ft. wide at maturity, making it an excellent choice for areas with limited space.

'Steeds'. A dense, upright grower that reaches 6–8 ft. tall and 4–6 ft. wide. Excellent as a hedge.

Ilex glabra (inkberry holly)

A hardy native found in natural habitats from eastern Canada to the southeastern and midwestern U.S., inkberry holly has a much different appearance from most traditional holly species. It has smooth, lush, linear, dark green leaves with no spines. It bears a small, jet black fruit in the fall, which will persist most of the winter. This species is a very useful hedge or screening plant that can be left natural or trained formally, depending on your needs.

Inkberry holly is an extremely adaptable plant that is able to grow in a variety of landscape situations, from a shady woodland to a hot, dry sunny location near the seashore. In the garden inkberry holly performs best in acidic, well-drained, loamy soil and full sun or partial shade, but it is quite adaptable.

Inkberry holly is one of the few hollies to spread by underground shoots forming large masses. It can be used effectively as a hedge, screen, mass planting, or foundation planting. Well-established plants can reach 6–8 ft. tall and wide. Hardy from Zones 4–10.

© Vincent A. Simeone

Mounded, dense shape of inkberry holly

© Bruce Curtis

Lush foliage of inkberry holly

NOTABLE VARIETIES

Many of the numerous recent inkberry holly cultivars are excellent additions to the garden.

'Compacta'. This slower-growing variety will not grow as large as the species, so it is more suitable for a smaller garden setting and as a formal hedge.

'Nigra'. Featuring dark green foliage, it is also relatively compact.

'Shamrock'. Like 'Nigra', 'Shamrock' is somewhat compact with dark green foliage and dense habit.

Ilex x meserveae (blue holly, Meserve holly)

Mrs. F. Leighton Meserve of Long Island, New York, produced the Meserve hybrid hollies in the early 1950s. To create these hybrids, Mrs. Meserve crossed the low-growing prostrate holly (*Ilex rugosa*), known for its cold tolerance and shrubby habit, with the English holly (*I. aquifolium*), possessing luxurious, glossy foliage.

Blue hollies have small, dark green leaves and deep purple stems. The leaves have a distinct leathery texture. Many of the blue holly varieties grow 8 ft. or more wide and high, developing into a thick mass of stems and leaves. Dragon Lady is the exception, with an upright, pyramidal habit to 15 ft. high. Blue hollies have bright red fruit that is rather attractive against the dark canvas of the foliage.

Because of their shrubby habit, blue hollies are excellent as formal or informal hedges and screens. Like most hollies, blue hollies are quite tolerant of pruning. They are especially effective in cooler climates, such as the northern and midwestern United States. They are best suited to Zones 5–7 but will tolerate certain parts of Zone 4, as well, if sited and in a protected location.

These hybrids do not perform particularly well in warmer climates that have excessive heat and humidity.

Since the 1960s many garden varieties have emerged, including 'Blue Boy', 'Blue Girl', 'Blue Prince', 'Blue Princess', China Girl ('Mesog'), and Dragon Lady ('Meschick'). Some are hybrids of different species from the two Mrs. Meserve first crossed.

Ilex opaca (American holly)

American holly, like English holly (*Ilex aquifolium*), will grow tall and should be sited where it has plenty of room. American holly has dull or semi-glossy, green, spiny leaves and a dense, pyramidal growth habit with strong lateral branches. The red berries also have a dull sheen but are nevertheless quite conspicuous clustered along each stem. As American holly matures, it develops smooth, light brown or gray bark with rough-textured accents.

American holly is very durable in the landscape and can tolerate a variety of soil types and levels of exposure to light, wind, salt spray, and heat. American holly is one of the most tolerant of all *Ilex* species to pruning. It prefers moist, well-drained, acidic soil and full sun or partial shade but is very adaptable. Although a slow grower, American holly will eventually reach 30–40 ft., with about a third the spread.

American holly is a large-growing evergreen and can serve as a large screen, with its tall, dense growth habit and broad, thick leaves. It is versatile and can also be used as a specimen or a formal or informal hedge, and it is adaptable as a woodland plant or in an exposed, sunny landscape. Hardy from Zones 5–9.

NOTABLE VARIETIES

There are dozens of American holly cultivars.

'Canary'. This yellow-fruited form will complement the red-fruited varieties very well.

'Dan Fenton'. This variety is an excellent choice, with lustrous foliage, pyramidal habit, and showy fruit.

'Jersey Knight'. This male clone is also an excellent type similar to 'Dan Fenton' with beautiful foliage.

'Jersey Princess'. Here is yet another great American holly sharing the characteristics of 'Jersey Knight', but it is a female clone. Both have a dense growth habit.

Ilex pedunculosa (longstalk holly)

An unusual Asian species, longstalk holly has somewhat of a tropical look in the garden; it resembles the popular tropical houseplant *Ficus benjamina*. Its smooth, wavy, green leaves have no spines, and its dense, upright growth habit stands out in the landscape. This species can be trained into a tree reaching 20 or more ft. in height. Longstalk holly produces deep red fruits attached to the branches by long stems.

Longstalk holly is rather slow growing and may be difficult to obtain in commerce, but it is well worth the effort. Few broadleaf evergreens have such grace and elegance. It is truly an exceptional evergreen for the plant collector with a keen eye for the unusual.

This cold-hardy species is ideal in northern climates and performs best in Zones 5–7. Longstalk holly is equally effective as a single specimen or in groupings. If used as a screen, it should be planted and maintained informally.

© Vincent A. Simeone

Mature American holly in the landscape

© Bruce Curtis

Lustrous foliage of 'Dan Fenton' holly

Ilex vomitoria (Yaupon holly)

Yaupon holly looks similar to Japanese holly, with delicate, thin, glossy foliage. Yaupon holly is very tolerant of hot, dry or humid climates, though. Both it and 'Burford' holly (*Ilex cornuta* 'Burfordii') do better than Japanese holly in the southern United States. The species name was derived from how this holly was utilized by Native Americans, who would make a tea from the leaves that would induce vomiting. They felt this cleansed their body and soul.

Yaupon holly assumes different forms, depending on the cultivar chosen. Typically, the species will form a dense, mounded habit, reaching 6 ft. by 6 ft. Its cultivars, though, can range from dwarf, dense habits to upright or weeping habits. This fast-growing evergreen is often used as formal or informal hedges and screens. Established specimens develop small, deep red, translucent berries, which ripen in the fall. Hardy from Zones 7–10.

NOTABLE VARIETIES

'Compacta'. This is an excellent variety with dense, compact growth habit and dark green, glossy leaves.

'Katherine'. This rather rare form offers striking yellow berries and a graceful, upright habit.

'Pendula'. This variety is another interesting form of Yaupon holly, with a vertical main trunk and strongly weeping lateral branches.

OTHER *ILEX* HYBRIDS

Let's quickly look over a few more of my favorite hybrid hollies. These will all function great in the landscape as living screens and hedges or for other purposes.

© Bruce Curtis

Smooth foliage and long-stalked berries of longstalk holly

© Vincent A. Simeone

Dense, upright habit of longstalk holly

Ilex × attenuata 'Foster #2'. This is a rather common holly in the southern United States because of its adaptability to heat and humidity. Foster's holly has slender, glossy leaves; bright red fruit; and an upright, densely conical shape. Mature specimens will reach 20–25 ft.. 'Longwood Gold' offers excellent dark green foliage and golden yellow fruit. Hardy from Zones 6–9.

Ilex × koehneana. The Koehne holly is a rather underutilized evergreen with large, lustrous, dark green leaves and large, red fruit. Mature specimens can reach 20–25 ft. in height. If you want something big and bold in the landscape, this hybrid will deliver. Besides its size, it has a distinct presence because of its coarse texture. 'Ajax', 'Chieftan', and 'Wirt L. Winn' are a few select cultivars available in the nursery trade. Hardy from Zones 7–9 and, with protection, possibly the warmer parts of Zone 6.

Ilex × 'Mary Nell'. This beautiful holly has shiny, thick leaves and deep red fruit in the fall and winter. The foliage makes this cultivar one of the best hollies available—and one of my favorites. The dense, upright habit reaches 10–20 ft., making 'Mary Nell' holly excellent as a screen for sun or shade. It is hardy from Zones 6–9, but it needs protection in colder climates of Zone 6.

Ilex × 'Nellie R. Stevens'. This robust hybrid between Chinese holly (*I. cornuta*) and English holly (*I. aquifolium*) offers lush, deep green leaves and reddish orange berries. 'Nellie R. Stevens' is one of the best hollies for warmer climates, and it thrives in the heat and humidity of the southern United

© Vincent A. Simeone

Red, translucent fruit of Yaupon holly

© Vincent A. Simeone

Yaupon holly pruned formally

States. It grows remarkably fast and can reach 25 ft. tall, with a dense, pyramidal habit. This plant is excellent as a screen or a specimen plant, but it does need room to grow. Hardy from Zones 6–9.

{ *Illicium floridanum*
Florida anise-tree

Florida anise-tree is an evergreen shrub offering an upright, dense growth habit and reddish purple flowers in spring. The unusual, star-shaped flowers have many petals and transform into star-shaped fruits in the fall. While *Illicium* is not overwhelming in flower, the individual flowers up close are quite interesting. Florida anise-tree also provides nice foliage texture, displaying medium- to dark-green leaves. It can make a rather handsome mass planting or screening plant. Individual plants grow 6–10 ft. or more in height, with a similar spread, but it usually stays smaller in colder climates.

This flowering shrub thrives in very moist, well-drained, organic soil and is partial shade. In full sun it may turn yellowish green or become damaged from too much exposure. Occasional maintenance pruning in early spring will keep this plant dense and compact.

Florida anise-tree, although considered an ornamental for southern gardens, will grow in hardiness Zones 6–9. It is an excellent foliage plant for shade gardens, for mass plantings, and as a screen or an informal hedge. The leaves have a strong aromatic smell when bruised and are supposedly repellent to deer.

© Vincent A. Simeone

Shiny foliage of 'Mary Nell' holly

© Vincent A. Simeone

Orange berries of 'Nellie R. Stevens' holly

NOTABLE VARIETIES

'Alba'. An interesting white flowering form, it has all the same attributes of the species.

'Halley's Comet'. A floriferous selection with deep red flowers and dark green foliage, this variety is effective in groupings in shady areas of the garden.

OTHER *ILLICIUM* SPECIES

Several other species of *Illicium* besides *I. floridanum* have shown garden merit, too. Small anise-tree (*I. parviflorum*) grows larger than *I. floridanum*, and Japanese anise-tree (*I. anisatum*) is a bit less cold hardy, growing from Zones 7–9. Both species display lush foliage and small, yellowish green flowers. These species are quite heat tolerant and can be used effectively in southern gardens.

{ *Kalmia latifolia*
Mountain laurel

Mountain laurel is a beautiful native shrub growing from eastern Canada to the southern and midwestern United States. In addition to its native range in our forests, mountain laurel is a very valuable ornamental for the garden. Because of its dense habit and adaptability, mountain laurel can function very effectively as a screen or an informal hedge. I would not recommend using this large shrub as a formal, pruned hedge or screen, though.

Mountain laurel has a naturally dense, mounded habit; too much pruning would compromise its natural beauty and flowering potential. Typically, this

© Vincent A. Simeone

Florida anise-tree in bloom

© Vincent A. Simeone

Spreading habit of Florida anise-tree

native shrub can reach 8–12 ft. tall and wide, but it is quite variable. Although mountain laurel is a relatively slow grower, it offers lush foliage, showy pastel flower clusters, and a dense growth habit. In spring rounded clusters of white-, pink-, or rose-colored flowers open. Each individual flower bud is star shaped, and collectively, the flowers create a spectacular floral display. See the Notable Varieties section for even more diversity in flowers, habit, and usage.

Mountain laurel prefers moist, well-drained, acidic soil and full sun or partial shade. It is quite adaptable, though, and will tolerate a variety of soils and light exposure levels—even drought. Although it prefers organic matter in the soil, it is still very important that the soil also be very well-drained. Plants situated in poorly drained, heavy clay soils will not perform well.

Mountain laurels are also very tolerant of pruning. Overgrown or poorly shaped shrubs can easily be rejuvenated by severe pruning, down to about 12 in., in early spring. Later in spring new growth will emerge from hidden growth buds present along the stems. This type of pruning often needs to be done on older plants that have been neglected for years. The result: a compact, vigorous plant more functional as a screen or an informal hedge.

Mountain laurel is an ideal woodland shrub for shade and is also effective in small groupings, in foundation plantings, and as a screening plant. If used as a hedge, it should be left informal so it may develop into a mounded shrub. Hardy from Zones 4–9.

© Vincent A. Simeone

Showy pink flowers of mountain laurel

© Vincent A. Simeone

Mounded habit and flower display of mountain laurel

NOTABLE VARIETIES

Extensive breeding since the 1960s has produced many exceptional garden varieties of mountain laurel with dense growth habits and blooms in a variety of colors. Many are available for the home garden, where their compactness makes them especially good for foundation plantings, low screens, and informal hedges. They range in color from white to pink to deep red. Some of the more recent varieties offer a striking, two-tone, banded coloration. The varieties listed here are a modest representation of available selections.

'Carousel'. The interior of the flowers offers a very striking, bright purplish cinnamon coloration.

'Minuet'. This mountain laurel has a dwarf growth habit and thin, glossy leaves. The pink buds open to creamy white flowers with deep maroon bands.

'Olympic Fire'. Its red buds open to vivid pink flowers.

'Raspberry Glow'. Deep red buds open to raspberry pink flowers.

'Sarah'. This variety has striking red flower buds that open to reveal deep pink flowers.

{ *Leucothoe fontanesiana*
Drooping leucothoe

Drooping leucothoe is a common native evergreen shrub that is related to rhododendrons and azaleas (*Rhododendron* spp.). Sometimes called fetterbush, it offers dark, glossy, green foliage and a graceful growth habit. The smooth, pointed leaves and graceful stems provide a beautiful cascading effect. Drooping leucothoe grows 3–6 ft. wide and several feet high. In spring delicate white, fragrant, urn-shaped flowers

© Vincent A. Simeone

Low, spreading habit of drooping leucothoe

hang from the bases of the leaves. Upon the arrival of colder temperatures in winter, the leaves often turn a striking burgundy purple color.

As a relative of rhododendron and inhabitant of the forest, drooping leucothoe thrives in moist, acidic, organic, well-drained soils. This plant does best if sited in a cool, partially shaded area of the garden. While partial shade is best, leucothoe will also tolerate dense shade. Leucothoe may be grown in full sun, though, provided it can be protected from high winds and is provided with mulch and adequate moisture. Selective or renewal pruning should be done in early spring. In general, removing the oldest stems every few years will keep older plants vigorous and dense.

Leucothoe is very effective in woodland gardens and can also be used in mass plantings with rhodo-

© Vincent A. Simeone

'Scarletta' foliage in spring

dendrons and azaleas. As a screen it should be used as an informal hedge or a low-level screen to hide the base of a structure or ground-level object. Hardy from Zones 5–8 and, with protection, Zone 4.

Truly a great shade-loving plant.

NOTABLE VARIETIES

'Girard's Rainbow'. This variety has interesting combinations of green, white, and pink in the leaf. It is a nice accent plant for adding interest to a bland area of the garden.

'Scarletta'. The new growth emerges glossy scarlet red and matures to deep green. The leaves turn brilliant burgundy red in winter.

{ *Ligustrum* spp.
Privets

Privets can be found in many different landscape applications, from formal hedges to large, informal screens to single specimens. The common California privet (*Ligustrum ovalifolium*) and Amur privet (*L. amurense*) tend to be semi-evergreen or deciduous, depending on the climate. While these and other deciduous species are quite functional and can be trained into impressive hedges, I'd like to offer a couple of evergreen species that, like the other privets, provide structure and function in the landscape.

Ligustrum japonicum (Japanese privet)

Japanese privet is truly evergreen and offers deep green, waxy leaves and a dense growth habit. The thick, lustrous leaves are really striking. Although I have nothing personal against the California and Amur privets, they are quite overused in many regions of the United States, and this species offers a nice alternative as a screen or a hedge.

Japanese privet has a bold, coarse texture, which catches the eye throughout the year. In spring spikes of creamy white, fragrant flowers form and persist for several weeks. Older specimens exhibit a smooth, gray bark, which adds to the year-round interest.

In addition to its aesthetic value, Japanese privet offers great function as a hedge or a screening plant. Plants can reach 6–12 ft. tall, with a similar spread, or can be kept smaller with regular judicious pruning. Japanese privet can be trained as a small tree, which would make it effective as a tall screen, or pruned into a formal or informal hedge. In either case the thick, lustrous leaves and fragrant flowers make Japanese privet a great addition to the garden. It can also be used in containers, in foundation plantings, or as a single specimen.

Japanese privet prefers moist, well-drained soil and full sun or partial shade. It is remarkably heat and drought tolerant once established in the landscape. This plant is also very adaptable to various types of soils and tolerant of salt and pollution. Hardy from Zones 7–10.

Ligustrum lucidum (Chinese privet)

Somewhat similar to Japanese privet (*Ligustrum japonicum*), the Chinese privet (*L. lucidum*) is also very useful as a hedge or screen. It is slightly less hardy, though, and more reliable in the warmer parts of Zone 7 through Zone 10. It offers an upright, spreading habit and thick, glossy leaves—hence its other common names, waxleaf privet and glossy privet. Chinese privet is very effective when limbed up and trained as a multistemmed tall shrub or small tree. It grows larger than Japanese privet, reaching heights of 20–25 ft.

{ *Loropetalum chinense* Chinese fringe-flower, Chinese loropetalum

Loropetalum, a finely textured evergreen shrub with a loose, open form, will grow as high as 12 ft. and as wide as 6–8 ft. Due to its spreading habit of horizontally arranged branches, though, it can also function as a screen or a hedge. The frilly, straplike flowers of Chinese fringe-flower, arranged in small clusters along each stem, resemble those of its close relative the

© Vincent A. Simeone

A grouping of Japanese privets

© Vincent A. Simeone

Rich, glossy leaves of Japanese privet

witchhazel (*Hamamelis* spp.). There are both white- and pink-flowered forms of *Loropetalum*, and both bloom prolifically beginning in late winter into spring, then continuing sporadically throughout the summer. The green-leaved varieties have fragrant flowers that are white or yellowish. In general the pink-flowered types are showier than the white-flowering ones; what's more, their leaves are dark green with burgundy, red, or copper tints, depending on the selection.

Chinese loropetalum performs best in rich, organic, acidic soil with good drainage, but it is very adaptable to various soil types. It prefers partial shade but will also thrive in full sun with adequate moisture. *Loropetalum* tolerates regular pruning and can easily be trained as a formal or informal hedge. Drought tolerant once established, it grows best in the southern parts of Zone 7 to Zone 10.

There seems to be great debate of how large Chinese loropetalum can grow, and much of this depends on the variety. On average the shrubs grow 6–12 ft. tall and wide. In addition to this charming, graceful ever-green shrub being used as a screen or a hedge, it can be effective in foundation plantings, as a backdrop in a shrub border, or as a companion plant to herbaceous perennials.

NOTABLE VARIETIES

L. chinense var. *rubrum* 'Blush' and 'Burgundy'. 'Blush' and 'Burgundy' are two named pink-flowered forms with reddish maroon leaves introduced in the early 1990s. Today they are among the most popular flowering shrubs in the southeastern United States.

© Vincent A. Simeone

Loropetalum in flower

© Vincent A. Simeone

Loropetalum in a mass planting (right)

'Zhuzhou Fuchsia'. This garden variety offers black-ish maroon foliage, bright pink flowers, and an upright habit—a combination that can be quite stunning in the landscape.

Magnolia grandiflora
Southern magnolia

Southern magnolia is a native tree found in the warmer climates of the southern United States. Sometimes called evergreen magnolia or bull bay, it is among the most beautiful broadleaf evergreens in the landscape, providing an eye-catching, bold texture. The large, glossy, dark green leaves and upright, dense growth habit make it ideal as a large screen. Although it has long been a favorite in southern gardens, several new varieties of this plant also grow in colder areas of the United States, including Zone 5.

In addition to the dark green leaves, select varieties display a rusty brown coloration to the leaf undersides, which adds an interesting contrast. The broad, upright, and typically pyramidal growth habit has a distinct presence in the landscape. Southern magnolia will flower later than most deciduous and evergreen magnolias, with large, fragrant, white flowers emerging in summer. Flowers can range from 8–12 in. in diameter and emit a sweet, lemony fragrance. Large, cone-like fruit ripens in the autumn and often persists through the winter. As the fruit ripens, small capsules open, exposing bright red seeds.

Southern magnolia is a resilient tree, preferring moist, well-drained, acidic soils and full sun or partial shade but tolerating less-than-optimum conditions.

© Vincent A. Simeone

Southern magnolia used as a screen

© Vincent A. Simeone

'Little Gem' foliage

Southern magnolia also tolerates poor soil, including heavy clay and sandy loam soils. In northern climates Southern magnolia can be planted in full sun or partial shade, but it should be protected from desiccating winds.

Southern magnolia can develop into a large tree, especially in warmer climates, and it must be given ample room to grow. It can be used as a tall screen along a house or large building. Mature specimens can grow 60 ft. high or more in the South, although the trees remain much smaller in colder climates. Southern magnolia can also be used as a single specimen or in informal groupings. Hardy from Zones 6–9, but several varieties have shown hardiness to Zone 5.

NOTABLE VARIETIES

'Brackens Brown Beauty'. This excellent selection has deep green, glossy foliage, with a rusty brown color and rough texture on the foliage underside.

'Edith Bogue'. This is one of the most popular and cold-hardy varieties of Southern magnolia.

'Little Gem'. A dwarf variety, it nevertheless reaches up to 20 ft. tall.

{ *Nandina domestica*
Heavenly bamboo

Although its common name is heavenly bamboo, this shrub is not related to the aggressive bamboo plants known throughout the world. Heavenly bamboo, a native of China, forms a rather neat clump of long, thin stems that reach 6–8 ft. The clumps of growth will spread by underground stems, but it is not usual-

© Vincent A. Simeone

Upright, shrubby habit and fruit clusters of heavenly bamboo

© Vincent A. Simeone

Low hedge of heavenly bamboo with lacy foliage

ly invasive in the landscape. Although heavenly bamboo is not considered a typical screening plant, it can be effective in groupings and informal plantings as a low or medium screen. There are many cultivated varieties of heavenly bamboo, from dwarf, low-growing varieties to taller, upright varieties.

The shiny leaves are made up of many small leaflets, collectively forming a fine, lacy appearance. The new growth ranges from coppery to pinkish red, aging to a soft blue-green. The foliage forms dense, flat-topped clusters at the end of each branch and in winter turns beautiful shades of reddish green. In spring the small, white flowers form at the ends of the stems. While not overwhelming, the bright red fruit clusters that ripen in autumn and persist through winter are quite attractive.

An older heavenly bamboo may need to be pruned regularly to ensure that dense growth forms at its base. This plant in general does need regular pruning every few years to remove old, thick stems. Selective removal of such stems will produce a healthier, more vigorous, and densely growing plant. An unpruned shrub would become tall and leggy and would lose its dense habit over time, making it ineffective as a screen. Pruning should be performed in late winter or early spring, while the shrub is still dormant.

Heavenly bamboo is remarkably durable and versatile in the landscape. It grows in a variety of soils and levels of light exposures and is especially tolerant of dense shade. For best results heavenly bamboo should be planted in groupings in full sun or partial shade and in moist, well-drained soil. In too much shade it is difficult to keep plants dense and branched to the ground. Hardy from Zones 6–9.

Osmanthus heterophyllus
Holly osmanthus

Holly osmanthus, also known as false holly, is a tall, spreading shrub or small tree that has spiny, holly-like foliage but is actually related to lilac and forsythia. The dark, rich-green, smooth foliage has spiny edges. Small, inconspicuous, creamy white flowers open in the autumn and may persist into early winter. The sweet fragrance of the flowers can be quite potent. Holly osmanthus does not bear ornamental fruit like true hollies, though.

Holly osmanthus has a shrubby, upright growth habit at youth but develops a spreading, rounded habit as it matures. Individual plants can grow 8–20 ft. tall. Holly osmanthus prefers well-drained, acidic soil and full sun or partial shade, but this species is also very tolerant of poor soils, drought, and dense shade.

Holly osmanthus is very tolerant of pruning and is very effective as a hedge or tall screen. Selective pruning every few years will keep plants vigorous and dense. If left unpruned, holly osmanthus can become rather ungainly over time. It works best as an informal hedge or screen, with selective maintenance pruning every few years. Holly osmanthus is not particularly fast growing, so unless you're training it as a formal hedge, significant pruning is often not needed regularly. Hardy from Zones 6–9.

NOTABLE VARIETIES

'Goshiki'. This variety is striking, with a swirled or speckled pattern of variegation on the foliage. This selection is very effective as an accent in a partially shaded area of the garden, but it is rather slow growing and semi-dwarf, so it will be effective only as a low screen or hedge.

'Gulftide'. A compact form with dark green, glossy, and extremely spiny leaves, 'Gulftide' will reach 10–15 ft. at maturity, with less of a spread.

'Variegata'. This upright, slow-growing variety has creamy white leaf margins.

OTHER *OSMANTHUS* SPECIES

Several other species of *Osmanthus* are ideal for the warmer parts of Zone 7 through Zone 10, making them very useful in the southeastern United States.

Spiny, lustrous foliage of holly osmanthus

Speckled leaves of 'Goshiki'

Devilwood (*O. americanus*), Fortune's osmanthus (*O. × fortunei*), and fragrant tea olive (*O. fragrans*) are excellent evergreens for warmer climates and can be used effectively in a wide variety of landscape situations.

{ *Photinia* spp.
Photinias

Evergreen photinias are tough, versatile flowering shrubs prevalent in many landscapes across the U.S. and Canada. The species primarily found in the southeastern United States is *Photinia × fraseri*, red-tip photinia. While disease problems and overuse have been an issue with this plant, the rounded white flower clusters in spring and brilliant red, glossy, evergreen foliage of new growth keeps us coming back for more.

'Kentucky' is a variety that has shown reasonably good resistance to a leaf spot that can typically wreak havoc on most red-tip plantings. Red-tip photinia is a very adaptable shrub, growing in very poor soils, shade, and exposed sites with admirable performance. This evergreen can take regular pruning and is used as a formal or informal screen or hedge. When choosing this plant, be sure to plant the disease-resistant variety.

Chinese photinia, *Photinia serrulata,* is an excellent species that is more resistant to leaf spot, which is usually contracted by red-tip photinia. This handsome large shrub has large clusters of white flowers in spring and rich, glossy leaves. The showy flowers can emit a foul smell and should be admired from a distance. The overall growth habit is upright and rounded. While mature plants can exceed 20 ft., they can also be used as smaller hedges and tall screens, depending on the pruning method chosen. Hardy from Zones 6–9, while red-tip photinia is hardy from Zones 7–9.

© Bruce Curtis

Green and variegated Japanese pieris in the landscape

{ *Pieris japonica*
Japanese pieris

Like rhododendron and mountain laurel, Japanese pieris is a very popular flowering shrub for the home landscape. The small, hanging flower buds are obvious in winter and develop into dangling bell-like flowers in early spring. The fragrant flower clusters last for several weeks in the cool spring weather. In addition to the white-flowering varieties, there are several pink-flowering varieties, which form clusters of noticeable pink or red flower buds in winter, before opening in spring. As the plants mature, they develop thick stems

© Vincent A. Simeone

'Valley Valentine' Japanese pieris in bloom

and rough, fissured, brown bark, which is very attractive in winter. Japanese pieris can grow up to 12 ft. tall, but in most residential landscape situations it can be maintained at 6–8 ft.

This flowering evergreen performs best in moist, well-drained, acidic soil and partial shade. It will not perform well in full sun or highly exposed, windy sites. Japanese pieris can be selectively pruned to maintain a dense habit. A poorly shaped plant can also be rejuvenated by being severely pruned to 12 in. in early spring; however, the shrub should be in good health to ensure that it can recover from this type of pruning.

Japanese pieris is effective in mass plantings, groupings, foundation plantings, woodland gardens, and as a screening plant. Japanese pieris is not appropriate as a formal hedge because shearing will reduce flower production and compromise its upright, naturally graceful growth habit. It is very effective in an informal planting as a hedge. Hardy from Zones 5–7, and with protection it will grow in Zone 4. Pieris is a rather deer-resistant plant.

NOTABLE VARIETIES

'Cavatine'. This later-blooming, dwarf form is exceptionally cold hardy.

'Dorothy Wycoff'. Striking, dark red flower buds open to pale pink flowers.

'Valley Valentine'. This variety offers dark green foliage and rich maroon flower buds, which open to deep pink flowers.

'Variegata'. A slow-growing, compact selection with creamy white leaf edges and white flowers, 'Variegata'

makes an excellent accent plant for a shaded area of the garden.

{ *Prunus* spp.
Cherry laurels

Ornamental cherries, plums, and apricots are common deciduous trees that are found in a wide variety of landscape situations. However, there are also several evergreen *Prunus* shrubs that are also quite functional and ornamental for gardeners who need a bold, dense screen. Below are two species that offer these desirable landscape qualities.

Prunus laurocerasus (cherry laurel)

Cherry laurel has broad, lustrous, dark green leaves and, in spring, white, upright flower stalks. This dense evergreen shrub is a close relative of the deciduous ornamental flowering cherries, being of the same genus. Plants can reach 10–15 ft. tall, with double the spread, at maturity but can be kept smaller with selective pruning. Although the select varieties discussed below are quite popular and widely available in commerce, the straight species is not readily available—but it should be. It is truly one of the most striking broadleaf evergreens, offering a coarse texture in the landscape.

Cherry laurel prefers shade, performing admirably in either partial or dense shade. Cherry laurel thrives in moist, well-drained, acidic, organic soil. A disease called shot hole fungus can cause small holes to develop in the leaves, but this problem is generally only cosmetic and not life threatening. Hardy from Zones 6–8.

Excessive pruning of cherry laurel should be avoided, since this could ruin its spreading growth habit. Selective pruning can be done in early spring while the plant is still dormant, or modest maintenance pruning can be performed right after flowering. It is imperative that cherry laurel be used in an informal planting rather than pruned formally; the Notable Varieties, especially, are best in informal groupings.

NOTABLE VARIETIES

Both of these varieties are very effective in mass plantings or small groupings in a shade garden. They can also be effective as a low screen or informal hedge.

'Otto Luyken'. This is a rather compact variety, growing only 3–4 ft. tall and 6–8 ft. wide.

'Schipkaensis'. This common selection has long, thin leaves and a wide-spreading growth habit. Established plants can grow 5–6 ft. tall, with twice the width.

Prunus lusitanica (Portuguese laurel)

Portuguese laurel, a lesser-known species than cherry laurel, has smooth, lustrous leaves and, in late spring, long, white, fragrant flowers. Reddish maroon fruits eventually ripen and also offer an interesting display. This rather handsome large shrub is a refreshing break from the norm and is worthy of selection for the home garden.

A mature plant reaches 10–20 ft. tall and wide. It seems to tolerate heat, full sun, and wind better than cherry laurel. Overall, it's a very effective shrub, especially in the mild climates of the Pacific Northwest region of the United States, and is hardy from Zones 7–9.

© Vincent A. Simeone

Lustrous leaves of cherry laurel

© Vincent A. Simeone

Dense, upright habit of cherry laurel

© Bruce Curtis

Spreading habit of 'Schipkaensis' cherry laurel

© Vincent A. Simeone

Cherry laurel in bloom

© Bruce Curtis

Grouping of 'Otto Luyken' cherry laurel in shade

© Bruce Curtis

Portuguese laurel foliage

{ *Rhaphiolepis umbellata*
Yeddo hawthorn

Yeddo hawthorn is a popular southern shrub with dark green, glossy evergreen foliage and 2–3 in. clusters of white or pink flowers in midspring. The bluish black fruit ripens in fall and persists into winter. New foliage is often gray-green, and leaves will have a purple tinge in winter.

This mounded shrub can reach 4–6 ft. tall and wide and offers a very dense habit. Yeddo hawthorn can be used as an informal or formal screen or hedge. It tolerates pruning but can often be maintained with occasional maintenance pruning rather than regular shearing. Yeddo hawthorn is also very effective in small groupings and as a foundation planting.

Yeddo hawthorn thrives in full sun or partial shade and well-drained, acidic soil. It is quite adaptable, also, being drought and heat tolerant and good for coastal areas with salt spray and wind. Hardy from the warmer parts of Zone 7–10.

{ *Rhododendron* spp.
Rhododendrons and azaleas

Rhododendrons are a valuable and diverse group of shrubs that offer masses of colorful blossoms in spring and summer. In addition, they can provide great function as a screen, an informal hedge, or a mass planting. Even in winter, rhododendrons liven up the garden with their lustrous evergreen foliage and dense growth patterns.

The name *Rhododendron* was derived from the Greek, meaning "rose tree." The more than eight hundred species are native to temperate areas of the Northern Hemisphere; the greatest number of species occurs in the Himalayas and extending east through other mountainous regions of the Far East and Indochina.

Rhododendrons do have specific cultural requirements. These needs include moist, acidic (pH about 5.5), organic, well-drained soil and partial shade. Because of this, rhododendrons thrive in moist, wooded areas under the light, dappled shade of deciduous and coniferous trees.

There are literally dozens of species and hundreds of varieties of rhododendrons commercially available that will function as screens and informal hedges. Rhododendrons are generally hardy from Zones 4–7, though that depends on the specific species or variety. At the end of each Notable Variety entry, the plant's coldest hardiness zone is given.

NOTABLE VARIETIES

These rhododendrons are just a small sampling of the exceptional varieties available in commerce. They are spring bloomers that also offer excellent foliage and dense evergreen habit.

'Aglo'. This medium-sized plant, a Weston Nurseries introduction, has light pink flowers and small, dark green leaves. Zone 4.

'Anita Gehnrich'. This midspring bloomer has showy deep pink flowers, fading to a paler shade of pink. The dark green, lustrous leaves and mounded, dense growth habit are also very attractive. Zone 5.

'Maxecat'. This is a hybrid between *Rhododendron*

'Roseum Elegans' rhododendrons in a mass planting

'PJM' rhododendron in bloom

maximum and *R. catawbiense*, two American natives. It offers good cold hardiness and heat tolerance as well as showy, pinkish purple flowers and glossy, dark green foliage. Zones 5–8.

'Percy Wiseman'. This beautiful mounded shrub has flowers opening a light pink with peach and fading to creamy white. Its habit is dense, and its foliage is dark green. Zone 6.

'PJM'. An older variety of rhododendron with bright purple flowers and an upright growth habit, 'PJM' has glossy, green leaves that turn deep maroon in the winter. Zone 4.

It is important to note that besides 'Aglo', there are several excellent additions to the garden that have been introduced by Weston Nurseries, such as 'Black Satin', 'Olga Mezzitt', and 'Weston's Pink Diamond'.

Rhododendron spp. (azaleas)

Azaleas, like their close relatives the rhododendrons, can function well as informal hedges. There are several key differences between azaleas and rhododendrons, including the shape of the flower and internal structure of the flower. Unfortunately, azaleas are often trained as formal hedges, but that type of pruning reduces flower production and compromises their graceful, layered growth habit.

Many azalea species and varieties are available today, but I still enjoy the old-fashioned Kurume hybrid azaleas, which offer many vibrant colors. I would also recommend azalea variety groups, such as the Back Acre Hybrids, Beltsville Hybrids, Glen Dale Hybrids, Girard Hybrids, and Robin Hill Hybrids. These groups represent azaleas that were developed for a specific climate or by a specific nursery or researcher. For cooler, northern climates, Poly Hill's North Tisbury Hybrids are good performers; for warmer, southern climates the Southern Indica Hybrids are preferable. With azalea hybrids the possibilities are endless.

NOTABLE VARIETIES

Here are just a few of the many azalea varieties worth researching. As with the previous such section, each entry ends with the coldest hardiness zone the variety can take.

'Coral Bells'. This low-growing shrub has delicate, coral pink flowers. Zone 6.

Delaware Valley. Featuring clear white flowers and bright green leaves, it grows 3–4 ft. high and wide. Zone 6.

Girard Crimson. With bright crimson flowers, this one is 3 ft. high and 4 ft. wide. It grows well in sun to part shade. Zone 6.

Girard Fuchsia. With deep fuchsia flowers, this

© Vincent A. Simeone

Informal habit of evergreen azalea

upright-growing shrub will grow 3–4 ft. in height. Zone 6.

Hino Crimson. The flowers are a brilliant red, and the growth habit is compact, to 3 ft. high and wide. There is an excellent bronzy maroon winter color on its leaves. Zone 5.

'Linda Stuart'. The flowers are a real eye-catcher. They emerge soft white with glowing, coral-orange edges. There is nothing else like it. The habit is low and nicely spreading, 3 ft. wide and tall. Zone 5.

'Nancy of Robin Hill'. Light pink, semi-double flowers provide a pleasant sight on this low-growing plant. Zone 6.

'Sherwood Red'. This is a dwarf plant with orange-red, single flowers. Zone 6.

'Sir Robert'. Its large, single, open-faced flowers vary from white to pink. It is a dense, compact, semi-dwarf grower. Zone 6.

Rhododendron catawbiense
(Catawba rhododendron)

The Catawba rhododendron is a native shrub of the southeastern U.S., with a range extending from Virginia to Georgia and Alabama. It has been widely used in hybridization. Its hardiness range is Zones 4–8.

NOTABLE VARIETIES

Here are a few *R. catawbiense* varieties and hybrids worth growing.

var. *album*. Pink buds open to pure white flowers.

'Catawbiense Album'. This cultivar is a hybrid of *R. catawbiense* and is different from the white variety *album*. Zones 4–7.

'English Roseum' ('Roseum Pink'). This offers light rose flowers, and a semi-compact growth habit. Zones 4–7.

'Grandiflorum'. Here's a rhododendron that is hardy to -25°F. It features distinctive lilac-colored flowers, an attractive plant habit, and good vigor. Zones 4–7.

'Purpureum Elegans'. This variety offers striking, bluish purple flowers. It has good cold hardiness and plant habit. Zones 4–7.

'Roseum Elegans'. This is one of the "old-fashioned" rhododendrons commonly known as "ironclads," a designation it earned by its tough, very hardy cultural adaptability. 'Roseum Elegans' is one of the most common and durable rhododendrons available. Zones 4–7.

'Scintillation'. This variety offers large, lush, glossy green foliage and showy, clear pink flowers in spring. Zone 5.

'Solidarity'. Its large, bold, pink flowers have a light purplish pink throat. The plant habit is dense and mounded when young, becoming large and open over time. Zone 5.

'Taurus'. In early spring the stunning large, deep-red flowers stand out against the deep-green foliage. Even before the flowers open, the dark, purplish red flower buds offer winter interest. Zone 6.

Rhododendron maximum (rosebay rhododendron)

Another excellent native rhododendron is the robust, large-leaved rosebay rhododendron, which is native from Canada to the midwestern and southern United States. Although not quite as widely available commercially as the Catawba hybrids (see *Rhododendron catawbiense*), the tough rosebay rhododendron offers great adaptability and function as a screen in the landscape. It can achieve great sizes in the landscape, from 8–20 ft. tall and wide. In large, open areas with ample shade and good drainage, this large evergreen shrub can make a great barrier planting. Just give it plenty of room!

In addition to its large, mounded, dense habit and long, dark green leaves, rosebay rhododendron displays showy flowers, ranging from rosy pink to creamy white, in late spring. Hardy from Zones 3–7.

© Vincent A. Simeone

Large red flower of 'Taurus' Catawba rhododendron

© Vincent A. Simeone

'Conoy' viburnum flowers and foliage

Rosebay rhododendron is often used in hybridization because of its pest resistance and ability to adapt to various soil and light conditions. 'Maxecat', a hybrid between *Rhododendron maximum* and *R. catawbiense*, is one good example of this.

{ *Viburnum* spp.
Evergreen viburnums

As a group, viburnums are quintessential flowering shrubs, offering great beauty and function in the landscape. The evergreen types of viburnums make excellent formal or informal hedges and screens because of their broad, lush foliage and dense branching habit. They are also remarkably adaptable to

varying cultural conditions and will grow in a wide variety of soil types and levels of light exposure. Here are a few evergreen viburnums suitable for the home landscape.

Viburnum × *burkwoodii* (Burkwood viburnum)

A semi-evergreen species, Burkwood viburnum has dark, glossy, green leaves most of the year. Essentially, in warmer climates it remains evergreen, but in the colder northern climates, it loses some or all of its leaves, depending on the severity of the winter. In a typical year, though, some foliage is retained even in the northern limits of its range, making it useful as a screening plant.

© Vincent A. Simeone

Lustrous foliage and showy flowers of Prague viburnum

© Vincent A. Simeone

Dense growth habit of lantanaphyllum viburnum

Burkwood viburnum develops into an upright, open shrub reaching 8–10 ft. tall, with a slightly smaller spread. In spring white, sweetly fragrant, rounded flowers develop, persisting several weeks. In flower this shrub will definitely get noticed. Hardy from Zones 4–8, but it benefits from protection in Zone 4.

NOTABLE VARIETIES

'Conoy'. This is a truly dwarf variety, with lustrous, glossy leaves and a dense growth habit. It grows to 5–6 ft. high, with an equal spread. Because of its compact growth habit, this shrub is ideal for the small landscape and can be used in groupings, in foundation plantings, and most importantly, as a low screen or informal hedge. 'Conoy' seems to be more reliably evergreen than the species. Its leaves are often tinged with a nice purple color in the winter.

'Eskimo'. This hybrid offers large, white flowers. They may lack fragrance, but they exhibit a spectacular display of color in spring, with clusters reaching 4–5 in. in diameter. 'Eskimo' tends to be semi-evergreen and has a dense, compact habit to 5 ft. tall and wide.

Viburnum × *pragense* (Prague viburnum)

The Prague viburnum is one of the most handsome of the evergreen viburnums. A cross between leatherleaf viburnum (*Viburnum rhytidophyllum*) and service viburnum (*V. utile*), it offers dark green, glossy, thick foliage year-round. The undersides of the leaves are silver, and they shimmer in the wind. The showy, flat-topped to rounded, creamy white flower clusters emerge in spring and offer a slight fragrance.

This shrub will grow up to 10 ft. tall, with a similar spread. Occasional selective pruning will keep it dense and productive but informal. For a more formal look, regular shearing will be needed. Prague viburnum is very effective as a screening plant, as an informal or formal hedge, or in a mass planting. Hardy from Zones 5–8.

Viburnum × rhytidophylloides (lantanaphyllum viburnum)

Lantanaphyllum viburnum is a hybrid of leatherleaf viburnum (*Viburnum × rhytidophyllum*) and looks similar. Lantanaphyllum viburnum has slightly smaller leaves than leatherleaf viburnum but sometimes a better flower and fruit display. It's hardy from Zones 5–8, but it will also grow in Zone 4 if sited in a sheltered location; it is a semi-evergreen shrub in cold climates.

Several *Viburnum × rhytidophylloides* varieties provide excellent foliage and flower interest in the landscape.

'Alleghany'. This variety has extremely dark green, leathery leaves; white flowers in spring; and bright red fruit, which turns black as it ages.

'Willowwood'. This durable shrub has beautiful green foliage and an upright habit with arching branches.

Viburnum rhytidophyllum (leatherleaf viburnum)

Leatherleaf viburnum offers large, thick, leathery, dark green leaves that can reach 7 in. long. The leaves have a sandpaper texture to them. The large, flat-topped,

© Vincent A. Simeone

Leatherleaf viburnum in flower

creamy white flowers open in spring and, though not overwhelming, are quite effective. This large, coarse evergreen grows to 15 ft. tall, with a similar spread. Leatherleaf viburnum has a distinctive, rounded appearance in the landscape and is suitable as a large, informal hedge or screen or in groupings. Hardy from Zones 5–7.

See also the entry for the somewhat similar *Viburnum × rhytidophylloides* (lantanaphyllum viburnum), a leatherleaf viburnum hybrid with smaller leaves but equally interesting flower and fruit interest. The hybrid also has both a bit more heat tolerance than its parent.

© Vincent A. Simeone

Leatherleaf viburnum foliage and flowers

Viburnum awabuki 'Chindo' (Chindo viburnum)

The Chindo viburnum is an evergreen viburnum with thick, highly glossy leaves and white, rounded to flat-topped flowers. Vigorous plants will produce bunches of bright red fruit that hang from the plant. Like many viburnum species, *V. awabuki* 'Chindo' produces better fruit displays when allowed to cross-pollinate, so plant in groupings. The dense growth habit and thick stems and leaves make this selection an excellent candidate as a hedge or tall screen.

Like most viburnums, 'Chindo' prefers moist, well-drained soil and full sun or partial shade. However, plants tend to perform best in a sheltered location protected from high winds and full winter exposure. 'Chindo' has an upright habit and can reach 10–15 ft. tall. Best in warmer climates from the southern part of Zone 7 to Zone 9.

Syringa meyeri, Meyer lilac

Deciduous and Semi-evergreen Shrubs

One of the main criteria for a good hedge or screen is the possession of a dense growth habit, which will block a view or hide an object. While evergreens serve this function very well, there are also many semi-evergreen and deciduous shrubs that provide excellent screening qualities. Even during the winter months, when many of these shrubs are leafless, their thick branching structures create impenetrable barriers.

⎨ *Abelia* spp.
Abelia

Abelia is a group of deciduous or semi-evergreen shrubs blooming in the summer. These rather easy-to-grow shrubs are versatile and are adaptable to various landscape situations, including small groupings, foundation plantings, perennial borders, and, of course, as effective informal hedges. The two species listed below are suitable for these applications.

Abelia chinensis (Chinese abelia)

Although related to glossy abelia (*Abelia* × *grandiflora*), being one of that hybrid's parents, Chinese abelia is a larger shrub, reaching 7 ft. in height, with an equal spread. Its leaves are medium green, and small, white, trumpet flowers are borne on new growth in profusion.

The flowers are fragrant and are smaller than those of glossy abelia. After the flowers fade, star-shaped flower stalks, also known as a calyces, remain and range from pale to medium pink.

This Asian species is adaptable to varying light exposure and soils but prefers full sun or partial shade and well-drained, acidic soils. This species is also slightly more cold hardy than glossy abelia.

Chinese abelia is ideal as an informal hedge or in a mass planting. This tough, cold-hardy flowering shrub grows in Zones 6–9. In Zone 5 it may get killed to the ground, but it will then regenerate from the roots in spring.

Abelia × *grandiflora* (glossy abelia)

Glossy abelia is a summer-blooming shrub with small, glossy leaves and a dense, mounded growth habit. The delicate, trumpet-like, white or pink flowers develop most of the summer and fall, making this plant a reliable late-season performer. The small, heart-shaped, glossy green leaves can turn a brilliant reddish maroon in fall and winter. The upright and spreading growth habit can reach 6 ft. in height, with a similar spread.

Abelia is quite adaptable, tolerating poor soil and considerable shade, but it prefers moist, well-drained soil and full sun. Abelia blooms on the current season's growth, so spring pruning before plants break dormancy is best. Tip pruning can be done to encourage a flush of new leaves and flowers. Selective or occasional rejuvenation pruning in spring will also stimulate flower production and create an informal hedge.

Abelia is an excellent informal hedge, foundation planting, or mass planting and is also very effective as a grouping. It can work well as a formal hedge, but it grows fast and will require regular shearing. Abelia has few pest problems if sited correctly and is an excellent butterfly-attracting plant. Its leaves are slow to emerge in the spring, but be patient because abelia will offer impressive foliage interest from summer until early winter. Even while nearly leafless in the early spring, abelia will function as an excellent hedge or low screen. Hardy from Zones 6–9.

NOTABLE VARIETIES:

'Canyon Creek'. This excellent accent plant has new leaves displaying a copper color that fades to yellow and finally green. The foliage later turns a bronzy rose color and is quite striking through the fall and winter in moderate climates.

'Edward Goucher'. This hybrid glossy abelia has lavender-pink flowers and lustrous green leaves that turn rich shades of reddish purple in fall. It is a very popular and widely used variety.

'Francis Mason'. This striking variety has bright yellow leaves that fade to yellow-green with age. It also produces light pink flowers but is essentially grown for its foliage. This plant can be effectively used in as an accent plant or in groupings in partial shade.

© Bruce Curtis

Glossy abelia in the landscape

'Rose Creek'. This dwarf plant only reaches 18 in. tall with twice the spread and features a profusion of pink flowers and reddish maroon winter foliage.

'Sherwoodii'. This dense, ground-hugging shrub grows to about 3 ft. tall. It is a very popular plant for foundation plantings, in groupings, as an edging plant, and as a low hedge.

Callicarpa spp.
Beautyberry

Beautyberries are unique shrubs that provide a beautiful show late in the season, as the cooler temperatures of fall arrive. In the landscape beautyberries often go unnoticed because of their generic appearance most of the year. But in late summer and early fall, they begin to make their presence known as clusters of small, pink flowers change to glossy purple fruit. By late fall this amazing shrub provides a spectacular display, as the succulent fruit glistens in the autumn sun.

Beautyberry performs best in full sun or partial shade. It also likes moist, well-drained soil but is quite adaptable. Selective pruning will keep the plant dense and healthy. Occasional rejuvenative pruning can be done in late winter or early spring by cutting the plant down to 12 in. This will encourage a dense, productive shrub.

Because of its ornamental fruit, beautyberry is ideal in groups, massing, informal hedges, and foundation plantings. This is a shrub that you want to site in a prominent location in the garden to show it off. Beautyberry is an excellent source of food for several species of songbirds. All species in the following discussions are hardy from Zones 5–8, except for Bodinier's beautyberry, which is hardy from Zones 6–8.

Callicarpa bodinieri var. giraldii 'Profusion' (Bodinier's beautyberry)

Bodinier's beautyberry has an upright growth habit, reaching 8–10 ft. in height. The large, dark purple fruit are a stunning addition to the garden. This selection is ideal for floral arranging since it produces the largest fruit of the beautyberries mentioned. Its leaves range from yellow to purple in the fall. Hardy from Zones 6–8, it is slightly less hardy than other cultivated beautyberries.

Callicarpa dichotoma (common beautyberry)

Common beautyberry is a compact grower with gracefully arching branches. This small shrub will reach 4–5 ft. in height, with a similar spread. During the summer soft-pink flower clusters line up along each stem. Once the flowers have been pollinated, bunches of bright purple berries emerge along the stems en masse. After the leaves fall off in autumn, the berries become most evident in the garden. The fruit will usually remain on the plants well into late fall, until the birds feast on them.

Because of its graceful, cascading growth habit, common beautyberry is very effective as an informal hedge or in a mass planting. The attractive stems can be harvested and used in floral arrangements, as well.

NOTABLE VARIETIES
'Albifructus'. This white-fruited form is very showy, with milky white fruit that glows in the landscape.

'Early Amethyst'. This early-fruiting form produces a profusion of small, lilac-colored fruit.

'Issai'. This unique variety sets an abundance of fruit as a young plant, providing almost immediate satisfaction.

Callicarpa japonica (Japanese beautyberry)

Japanese beautyberry is a large shrub growing 8 ft. or more in height with a violet-purple fruit in autumn. Japanese beautyberry has an upright, dense branching structure, making it a very useful garden plant.

NOTABLE VARIETY
'Leucocarpa'. This white-fruited form is usually showier than the purple-fruited form.

{ *Chaenomeles speciosa*
Flowering quince

This old-fashioned shrub has been cultivated for centuries and is now reemerging as a desirable ornamental flowering shrub. Flowering quince is useful as an informal hedge or screen because as it becomes established, it creates a dense thicket of branches that is impenetrable. The twigs are often spiny and form a mounded habit to 6–8 ft. in height and spread. The flowers vary from white to pink to deep red in late winter or early spring, persisting to midspring. They are arranged in clusters along the interior of the shrub. The smooth, green, apple-like fruit ripens in fall, reaching 2–3 in. in diameter and emitting a fruity fragrance. This edible fruit is quite tart and can be cooked to make preserves and jellies. New foliage on quince emerges a bronzy red color and changes to dark, glossy green.

Flowering quince performs best in full sun and moist, well-drained, acidic soil but is extremely adaptable. It is heat and drought tolerant and will adapt to most soil types. Selective pruning can be done in early spring to remove old, unproductive branches. These branches are generally pruned as close to the ground as possible. Occasional rejuvenation pruning, cutting the entire plant to 6–12 in. from the ground, will create a more compact, vigorous shrub that can be trained. Although this method will revitalize your shrub, it will take at least a year for the plant to reliably flower and fruit again. Light pruning to shape plants can also be done after flowering.

© Vincent A. Simeone

Flowering quince in flower

Flowering quince is excellent as an informal barrier hedge because of its spines and dense branching pattern. It can also be used in groupings, mass plantings, and shrub borders. Many gardeners plant it in the garden for early spring interest and to harvest the fruit in the fall. Zones 4–8; with specific siting in a protected location, possibly 9.

NOTABLE VARIETIES

'Apple Blossom'. The large, pale pink flowers are 2 in. in diameter.

'Cameo'. This variety features double, peachy pink flowers in profusion.

'Toyo-Nishiki'. This unique selection has a combination of white, pink, and red flowers.

© Vincent A. Simeone

Dense, spreading habit of buttercup winterhazel in winter

© Vincent A. Simeone

Buttercup winterhazel flowers

© Vincent A. Simeone

Buttercup winterhazel flowering in the landscape

{ *Corylopsis pauciflora*
Buttercup winterhazel

Although there are several winterhazels native to the United States, this species is native to Asia. Buttercup winterhazel is the most compact of the winterhazels, so it is suitable for the home landscape with limited space. Winterhazel is well known as an early-blooming shrub with a wide, spreading growing habit. The average size of this plant in the garden is 5 ft. tall, with a 6–8 ft. spread. This densely growing shrub creates such a thick-branching habit that it is hard to see through it even when it sheds its leaves in the fall. For this reason buttercup winterhazel is excellent as an informal hedge or in a grouping used as a screen.

In addition to its functional qualities, this delicate shrub provides a profuse display of early spring color in the garden that is rivaled by few plants. Buttercup winterhazel has showy yellow, fragrant flowers, which will persist for several weeks. The flowers appear in late winter or early spring, at a time when the garden is just waking up. After the flowers fade, small, pleated green leaves emerge, turning a beautiful golden yellow in the fall.

This unique shrub prefers, moist, organic, acidic, well-drained, soil and full sun or partial shade. Pruning should be kept to a minimum, as excessive pruning would disfigure the plant's beautiful growth habit. If the plant is not productive, selective pruning can be done in early spring to encourage new stems, which will flower the following year.

Buttercup winterhazel is very effective in woodland gardens, in mass plantings, or as a low screen or informal hedge. Many gardeners underestimate how wide this plant will grow, so remember to give it plenty of room. Planting shrubs at least 5–6 ft. apart is most beneficial. Hardy from Zones 6–8.

{ *Deutzia* spp. Deutzias

Deutzia is a reliable old-fashioned flowering shrub prized for its adaptability and ability to produce a profusion of showy spring flowers. The flowers range from white to deep pink, single or double, depending on the variety. In spring the cascading branches will be covered with a dense display of colorful flowers. In general, deutzia is most evident in spring, when it displays its masses of showy flowers. After flowering, deutzia's graceful growth habit is most evident as well as its lush, medium-green leaves. The growth habit is strongly upright or spreading. These versatile shrubs range in size from 4–8 ft. tall and are best when used as informal hedges or screens.

Deutzia is an easy plant to grow and will adapt to most soils, levels of light exposure, and landscape situations. Deutzia blooms on the previous year's growth, so maintenance pruning to keep the plant dense and productive should be done right after flowering. Shearing often ruins its graceful habit, so this form of pruning is not recommended. If a plant is in poor health, severe, nonselective pruning may be needed. In such a situation, the shrub can be pruned to 6 in., which will result in a flush of vigorous new vegetative growth the first season, followed by flowers the second season.

In general, deutzia is very effective as a mass planting, in a small grouping, as a background plant along a foundation, or as an informal hedge. Hardy from Zones 5–8.

Deutzia gracilis (slender deutzia)

Slender deutzia has a distinct mounded growth habit to 3 ft. in height and a spread of 3–4 ft. Although it is the smallest of the deutzias, it is very effective as an informal hedge or low screen. The attractive white flowers are borne on upright spikes in midspring, providing a great splash of midseason color. The small, deep-green, pointed leaves are typically tinged with shades of purple in the autumn.

Like many other deutzias, slender deutzia is easy to grow and adapts well to almost any landscape situation. It responds well to pruning, but that is usually not needed on a regular basis. Slender deutzia thrives in well-drained, moist soils and full sun but is remarkably tolerant of poor soil and shade. Pruning with pruning shears, not hedge shears, right after flowering will maintain a dense, neat grower. If neglected, this shrub may appear sparse or leggy, but an early spring pruning to 6 in. will quickly rejuvenate it. Slender deutzia has no major pest problems and is exceptionally drought tolerant, cold hardy, and adaptable to most soil types and levels of light exposure.

In addition to being suitable as an informal hedge, slender deutzia can also be utilized as an edging plant, in foundation plantings, and in small groupings. Hardy from Zones 4–8.

Deutzia scabra (fuzzy deutzia)

Fuzzy deutzia is a common species that has been a popular fixture in both American and European gardens for centuries. While its popularity has waned a bit in more recent history, interest has increased in this flowering shrub over the past decade. Below is a list of a few exceptional selections.

NOTABLE VARIETIES

'Flore-pleno'. Also known as just 'Plena', this attractive variety offers white, double flowers with an unusual ruffled look. This plant can reach 6–8 ft. in height and should be used as a background plant or in groupings.

'Pink Minor'. This is a fairly compact variety, to 3 ft. tall, with an equal spread. Its attractive light pink flowers and dense growth habit make this variety ideal in foundation plantings and mixed plant borders.

'Pride of Rochester'. The light pink, double flowers provide a nice show of soft pastel color.

© Vincent A. Simeone

Low hedge of slender deutzia in flower

Deutzia hybrids

There have been several key pink-flowering selections of deutzia that are a result of hybrids between several species. These selections offer a profusion of spring color and noticeable structure and texture in the landscape. Below are a few of my favorite varieties.

NOTABLE VARIETIES

D. × 'Magician'. A white stripe along the edge of the petal gives the individual deep pink flowers a beautiful two-tone coloration. This hybrid is excellent as a background plant or in groupings and effectively used as a backdrop in the perennial border.

D. × Pink-a-Boo ('Monzia'). This beautifully graceful grower has arching branches and waves of pink flowers.

D. × 'Rosalind'. This graceful shrub has an upright growth habit with arching branches to 5 ft. tall and deep pink flowers.

{ *Forsythia* × *intermedia*
Border forsythia

Border forsythia is one of the most well-known and recognizable flowering shrubs in gardens today. If used properly, it can develop into a very effective informal hedge or mass planting.

Without question, though, forsythia is the most misused of all deciduous shrubs that are appropriate as informal hedges. All too often we (present company excluded) butcher this plant in our quest to transform it from its graceful, informal habit into a formal, manicured hedge. I have also often witnessed forsythia formally pruned and shaped into teardrops, lollipops, and other unnatural forms. If left natural, the beautiful, arching branches cascade down to the ground in a very graceful manner, but that form is lost when the shrubs are pruned in a formal manner. Besides not letting the plants fully develop into their natural form, regular pruning will reduce flowering and could compromise plant health over time.

One of the motivations for pruning regularly is often the fact that forsythia is sited in a location that is too small, so it would overgrow its bounds without pruning. My advice in this regard is to carefully select an area of the garden where forsythia will have adequate room and to refrain from shearing or severe pruning on a regular basis.

© Vincent A. Simeone

Cascading habit and rosy pink flowers of 'Rosalind' deutzia

Border forsythia may be lightly pruned after flowering to reduce its size, though. Also, selectively removing older stems every few years promotes the growth of healthy new branches from the base of the plant. An occasional severe rejuvenation pruning in late winter or early spring will also renovate an unproductive shrub. Since forsythia blooms on the previous year's growth, flowers will be sacrificed for one year by a rejuvenation pruning. However, the gardener will be pleasantly surprised by the impressive display of color in the second season.

Forsythia is easily identified by the flush of golden yellow flowers in early spring. To many gardeners blooming forsythia signifies the unofficial start of spring. After the flowers finish, medium to dark green leaves emerge, providing lush vegetation all summer. The fall foliage color is variable and can change from yellow to shades of reddish purple.

Forsythia is a very adaptable shrub, tolerating varying types of soil, levels of light exposure, and even pollution. Well-drained, moist soil, though, provides optimum conditions for this plant to thrive. Border forsythia should be sited in full sun or partial shade and given plenty of room.

Border forsythia is a large, spreading shrub, easily growing 8 ft. tall and 12 ft. wide. A fast-growing plant, it flowers heavily even at a young age. Although border forsythia can overwhelm a small garden with its robust size, occasional selective pruning in late winter or early spring to remove older stems will keep it in scale, reducing the possibility of an overgrown planting.

In addition to informal hedges, forsythia can be used in groupings, mass plantings, and background plantings. Border forsythia is very effective in a home garden as an informal hedge, mass planting, and a barrier plant or screen. Once established, border forsythia creates such a thick, impenetrable barrier in the landscape, it will successfully camouflage just about anything, such as an old shed or an unsightly view of a neighboring house. It is best from Zones 6–8, but it may also grow in Zones 5 and 9 if sited correctly in a sheltered location.

NOTABLE VARIETIES

'Beatrix Ferrand'. This handsome variety offers large, golden yellow flowers in early spring. It is named after a famous American garden designer.

© Vincent A. Simeone

Border forsythia as an informal hedge

'Fiesta'. This variegated cultivar has interesting combinations of green and yellow in its leaves. This plant also has interesting red stems, so it works well as an accent in the landscape. It is a low grower.

Gold Tide ('Courtasol'). This compact, low-growing variety has medium-green leaves and profuse clusters of yellow flowers. It is an excellent plant as a ground-cover or in mass plantings.

'Lynwood'. This selection provides a brilliant display of yellow flowers and an upright growth habit. One of the most reliable varieties available, it originated in Ireland.

'Spring Glory'. This early-flowering type has bright yellow flowers.

{ *Kolkwitzia amabilis*
{ Beautybush

Beautybush has earned its name from the masses of beautiful pink, trumpet-like flowers that it displays in midspring. The large bunches of tightly arranged flowers transform into puffs of hairy fruit capsules late in the summer season. This upright shrub can grow 6–10 ft. tall and forms a dense branching habit. The small, medium-green, pointed leaves turn yellowish or tinged red in the fall. Because of its ultimate size, beautybush is effective as a tall informal hedge. It requires plenty of room and it can easily outgrow a space with limited room.

Beautybush is rather easy to grow and will thrive in moist, well-drained soils and full sun. It is very adaptable to varying soil types and pH levels, and it is drought tolerant once established. Regular selective pruning to remove older stems is recommended to maximize flower production and vigor. If an older shrub gets too overgrown, a severe pruning in the early spring will rejuvenate it, but flowers will be sacrificed for one year. However, flower production will improve over the next few years.

This large flowering shrub can be used as a stand-alone plant, in small groupings, or in a larger informal hedge planting. Since it forms a very dense mass of growth, it is very useful along a property line to ensure privacy. Hardy from Zones 4–8.

NOTABLE VARIETY

'Pink Cloud'. It has profuse masses of light pink flowers, which form a cloud of magnificent color.

© Vincent A. Simeone

Cascading habit and profuse flowering of beautybush

© Vincent A. Simeone

Pink, tubular flowers of beautybush

{ *Neillia sinensis*
Chinese neillia

Chinese neillia is an unusual and beautiful flowering shrub that is rarely encountered in the home landscape. It is sometimes found in the collector's garden, where it will complement other unusual garden treasures. Because of its dense, upright habit and zigzag branching pattern, *Neillia* is very useful as an informal hedge. The small groups of pink flowers dangle off the irregular-growing stems in midspring. The lush, deep green, serrated leaves provide excellent texture during the summer. The tightly arranged stems form a dense thicket that is interesting all year, especially when the shrub sheds its leaves in the fall. The bark on older, mature stems will exfoliate, adding another interesting dimension to this underutilized plant.

Neillia will grow to 6 ft. wide and tall but can grow larger in optimum conditions. The densely growing branches make it difficult to see through even during the winter months. This fast-growing shrub prefers moist, well-drained soil and full sun or partial shade. Pruning can be done soon after flowering to keep the plant dense and neat. However, selective pruning in early spring is best for stimulating healthy plant growth. *Neillia* is an adaptable plant but performs best in cooler climates of the northern United States.

Chinese neillia needs room but will function as a natural screen, informal hedge, or background plant and is most effective in a mass planting. Although this choice species is not readily obtainable, it can be acquired from a mail-order or specialty plant nursery.

The little trouble is worth it because *Neillia* will provide great function and beauty to the landscape. This plant is hardy from Zones 5–7.

{ *Philadelphus* spp.
Mockorange

Mockorange (*Philadelphus* spp.) is an old-fashioned shrub with a tall, dense habit, lush green foliage, and showy pure white, fragrant flowers. Mockorange can fill the surrounding area with a wonderfully sweet fragrance when in full bloom. Mockorange is extremely adaptable, tolerating a wide variety of soil types and light exposure. Below is a listing of several species and garden varieties worthy of consideration as an informal hedge or tall screen.

Philadelphus coronarius (sweet mockorange)

Sweet mockorange is an old-fashioned shrub that offers sweet, intoxicatingly fragrant white flowers in spring. The flowers make a pleasant combination with the dark green leaves. The reddish brown stems provide interest in the winter, especially against a blanket of snow. Like deutzia, viburnum, and other flowering shrubs, mockorange is suitable as an informal hedge because of its upright, dense growth habit.

This European native is quite adaptable but flowers best in full sun or partial shade and moist, well-drained soils. It will tolerate poor soils and considerable shade, but flower production will be reduced. Selective pruning in late winter is recommended to remove weak or older stems. If a shrub is too overgrown, a nonselective rejuvenation pruning can renovate it. However, it will take the sweet mockorange at least a year to regain a profuse production of flowers. Sweet mockorange will grow to 10–12 ft. in height, with a similar spread, but typically does not reach such large sizes until it gets quite old.

Sweet mockorange is best sited where you can enjoy the pleasant fragrance of the flowers. As an informal hedge, a line of sweet mockoranges can be sited along a property line or against a building with very effective results. In addition, sweet mockorange is suitable in mass plantings, in groupings, and as a single specimen. Hardy from Zones 4–8.

NOTABLE VARIETIES

'Aureus'. The foliage is striking yellow, fading to chartreuse yellow over time. The foliage color makes this variety ideal for an accent in a partly shaded area of the garden. It is generally very effective for brightening up a rather color-challenged area. This variety is more effective in cooler climates with less heat and humidity, where the leaf color is less likely to fade.

'Variegatus'. Creamy white leaf edges make this worthy shrub a good accent plant in a partially shaded area of the garden.

Philadelphus hybrids

Here are a few select mockorange varieties derived from several different species.

P. × *lemoinei* 'Innocence'. This variety comes from a hybrid and is one of the best mockoranges for fragrance. It is a unique selection, with leaves splashed with off-white variegation. It is good as an accent plant

for sunny or partially shaded areas.

P. 'Snowbelle'. A hybrid mockorange with a compact growth habit to 4 ft. tall, it features masses of fragrant, small, white, double flowers.

P. × *virginalis* 'Minnesota Snowflake'. This hybrid mockorange has white, double flowers with a ruffled appearance and pleasant fragrance.

{ *Physocarpus opulifolius*
Common ninebark

This North American native naturally grows from Quebec, Canada, to the eastern and midwestern United States, hence another common name, eastern ninebark. It is one of the most cold-hardy and durable flowering shrubs available in commerce. Ninebark has white or light pink flowers in mid- to late spring and medium-green leaves in the summer. Mature specimens offer winter interest since the bark on the older branches will peel off in brown sheets. Although it is not a particularly overpowering shrub in the landscape, there are several new varieties that offer striking foliage.

Ninebark, like viburnum and mockorange, is a very adaptable shrub, growing well in various soils. It is not pH dependent and can also tolerate poor, dry soil. It thrives in full sun or partial shade and moist, well-drained soil. Rejuvenation pruning to 12 in. in early spring will stimulate this shrub to grow several feet in one season. If left unpruned, ninebark can reach 10 ft. tall, but it can be maintained smaller with selective pruning. In such a case it is very effective as an informal hedge. Whether in groupings or as a single planting, ninebark will offer function as a screen as well as aesthetic value.

Ninebark has gained popularity over the past few years since several new varieties have emerged with purple or yellow foliage. These interesting "accent" plants should be pruned to 6 in. from the ground annually to encourage deep, intense colors. Like smokebush (*Cotinus* spp.), this plant functions well as a "cutback shrub," which requires severe, rejuvenation pruning of the plant down to 12 in. in late winter or early spring. Smokebush is also very useful in mass plantings, in shrub borders, and when mixed with perennials. If used as a cutback shrub, ninebark can be maintained as an informal hedge or low screen. Ninebark is an extremely cold-hardy plant, growing in Zones 2–7.

NOTABLE VARIETIES

'Dart's Gold'. This compact grower has golden foliage in spring, fading to a yellow-green over time. The plants grows 4–5 ft. tall, with a similar spread. It makes a very nice accent plant when mixed with dark foliage plants.

Diablo ('Monlo'). Its foliage is a deep purple in spring, fading to a purplish green as the leaves mature. The bold, robust leaves provide great texture and color in the landscape during the summer months. In hot, humid climates, often leaves start out deep purple in spring and fade to purplish green as the summer progresses. Still, it is a very hardy and useful accent plant in the right situation.

'Nugget'. Similar to 'Dart's Gold', 'Nugget' is another fine yellow-leaf form worth trying. It has a rather handsome compact growth habit.

{ *Rosa* spp.
Rose

It may be hard to believe, but even roses can be used as informal hedges. These would be not the traditional tea roses but the more modern introductions known as shrub roses. These plants offer beautiful summer blooms, improved pest resistance, and a dense, shrubby growth habit. While the flowers and fragrance of these newer shrub roses are not quite as flamboyant as those of tea roses, they still are quite impressive and very functional in the landscape.

There are several types of rose flowers, including a single type, which reveals the open center of the flower, and a double flower, which has a ruffled appearance. The flowers are coveted for their intoxicating fragrance, which few gardeners can resist. Rose hips are oval or globular fruits that can range in size and color when ripe but are usually red or orange in late summer and fall.

Although the beauty of roses is obvious, many varieties are susceptible to an assortment of diseases and pest problems, such as aphids, spider mites, midge, black spot, rust, and powdery mildew. Black spot, one of the most prevalent diseases of roses, causes small, black spots on the leaves. Badly infested plants may defoliate and, if healthy, will then produce new leaves. The severity of these common rose diseases depends on many factors, such as environmental conditions, rose variety, and even the region of the country the plant is growing in. For example, roses growing in the Pacific Northwest region of the United States may not have the same types or degree of disease and pest problems that you might encounter in the southeastern United States.

Although many rose disease and pest problems can be treated with chemicals, there are many more environmentally sound alternatives. Among them, the most effective is prevention through proper plant selection. Significant research has yielded dozens of exciting new varieties of landscape roses that offer shrubby habits, improved flowering characteristics, and impressive pest resistance. If pesticides are needed, though, careful research should be done to select the best product for a specific problem. Before using a pesticide, you should consult with a local county extension agent or other horticultural professional.

In general, roses require regular care to stay healthy and productive. However, the new, improved rose varieties available today are generally better landscape plants, offering pest resistance, cultural adaptability, aesthetic value, and superior landscape function. These attributes result in less maintenance and more enjoyment.

Most of the cultivated varieties discussed below are hardy to Zone 4–8, with a few exceptions. In addition, these low-growing or shrubby-type roses are excellent as low informal hedges, mass plantings, and foundation plantings and can be combined with herbaceous plants. They thrive in well-drained, moist soil and full sun but, once established, are reasonably tolerant of poor soil and drought conditions. Spring and/or fall fertilization and regular watering during the first few

seasons will also benefit shrub roses. They can be pruned in the spring to thin out older stems, leaving the younger, stronger stems to grow better.

NOTABLE VARIETIES

This is a modest offering of some of the more choice rose selections available for the home garden. Please note that whereas in most cases throughout this book cultivated variety names are listed with single quotes around each name (for example, *Rosa* 'The Fairy'), some trademarked or registered rose names are more common and identifiable on the market, and such names don't take single quotes. Therefore, several of the roses listed here indicate these more common trade or registered names first, with cultivated variety names in parentheses.

Alba Meidiland ('Meiflopan'). The large clusters of small, white flowers emit a slight fragrance. This low-growing plant, with a nice, cascading growth habit, reaches 2½ ft. tall by 6 ft. wide.

Bonica ('Mediopmonac'). This upright grower offers lush, dark green foliage and medium pink, double flowers. The plant grows into a dense, 4 ft. mound.

Carefree Delight ('Meipotal'). This hardy, compact grower provides attractive single, pink blooms all summer. The plant grows to 4 ft. tall, with a similar spread.

Carefree Sunshine ('Radsun'). This unique shrub has golden yellow flowers and a compact, dense, 3–4 ft. growth habit.

Carefree Wonder ('Meipitac'). A very popular variety, this has interesting shades of pink blended into

© Vincent A. Simeone

Knock Out roses as hedges

each semi-double flower. The dense, neat growth habit will reach 4 ft. in height.

'The Fairy'. A very reliable performer with delicate double pink flowers in mid summer and a dense, low growing habit. The glossy green leaves are also attractive and individual plants range in size from 2–3 ft. up to 4 ft. in height, with an equal or larger spread.

Knock Out ('Radrazz'). This excellent variety has a name that speaks for itself. Its hot pink blooms illuminate the garden with color. The floral display is quite dramatic. The beautiful, dark green foliage and dense growth habit make it ideal as an informal hedge. Recently, there have been several new introductions to the Knock Out series, including Pink Knock Out

('Radcon') and Blushing Knock Out ('Radyod'). These varieties offer medium pink or pale pink flowers.

R. chinensis 'Mutabilis'. A shrub rose to 6 ft. tall and wide, it has beautiful flowers that range from yellow to salmon to deep pink simultaneously. This plant also has very beautiful blue-green foliage but is susceptible to black spot. It is still a good performer and worthy of planting in the garden. Excellent in hardiness Zones 7 and 8.

Pink Meidiland ('Meipoque'). The pink, single flowers with white centers emerge in spring, and flowering will continue into the fall. The dense, upright growth habit will reach 4 ft. high and 2½ ft. wide. The red rose hips will persist, adding winter interest.

Scarlet Meidiland ('Meikrotal'). This variety provides clusters of small, scarlet red, double flowers in early summer, with blooming continuing through fall. This variety will grow 3 ft. high by 6 ft. wide and make a dense informal hedge or mass planting.

'Seafoam'. An older, established variety, 'Seafoam' features small, creamy white, double flowers in profusion beginning in early summer and continuing sporadically into the fall. This vigorous rose will grow 3 ft. high by 6 ft. wide, with a beautiful cascading growth habit.

Spiraea spp.
Spirea

Spiraea comprises a group of popular flowering shrubs that have been an important part of gardening since the late 1800s. Like forsythia, rhododendron, and lilac, spirea has earned the reputation as a hardy, colorful old-fashioned shrub. Spirea offers colorful spring and summer flowers, a dense growth habit, and beautiful smooth foliage. Although we don't often think of it as useful in hedges or screens, there are several spireas that can offer these qualities in addition to their multi-seasonal ornamental value.

Spirea is not without faults, possibly falling prey to several damaging insects, such as aphids, scale, and caterpillars. However, even with these potential problems, spirea exhibits remarkable resiliency. It performs best in full sun or partial shade and well-drained, loamy soils, but it tolerates all types of soils except those that are poorly drained. Depending on the species, spirea blooms in either spring or summer.

As a general rule, spring-blooming spireas should be pruned after flowering, and summer-blooming types should be pruned while the shrubs are still dormant in early spring. For this reason it is important to know which type of spirea you have growing in the garden. This information will also affect how you prune your spirea hedges for maximizing their effectiveness in the landscape.

Spirea offers versatility and can be used in mass plantings, foundation plantings, perennial borders, as low edging plants, and as formal or informal hedges. Even though it is deciduous, spirea has a dense branching habit, making it useful as a hedge. It is hardy from Zones 3–8, depending on the species.

Spiraea × *bumalda* (Bumald spirea)
It is difficult to imagine that this dwarf plant can be used as a hedge, but with proper training and care,

Bumald spirea can develop into a very functional low hedge. This shrub forms a dense mounded habit 3–4 ft. high, with a similar spread. The new leaves unfold reddish purple in spring and with age change to dark green. The small, flat-topped flower bouquets, ranging from light to deep pink, bloom in early to midsummer. Often plants sporadically bloom into the fall.

Bumald spirea is very adaptable but does best in well-drained, moist soil and full sun or partial shade. Because it flowers on the most current season's growth, pruning before the leaves emerge in the spring is recommended. A plant can be pruned down to 6 in., and then it will grow several feet in one growing season, including a display of a mass of flowers that first season. This type of pruning will also keep the plant dense and compact. Neglected plants that are not pruned each spring will eventually flop and open up in the center. After blooming, the flowers can be pruned off, which often encourages another flush of blooms.

Bumald spirea is very functional in the home garden and can be used in mass plantings, foundation plantings, and shrub borders. As an informal low hedge, it can line a walkway or patio or define a garden area. Hardy from Zones 3–8.

NOTABLE VARIETIES

'Anthony Waterer'. This popular variety is an improvement over the species, with the newest foliage tinged reddish purple and flower clusters rosy pink. In the autumn the foliage often displays attractive shades of red.

© Vincent A. Simeone

Low hedge of Bumald spirea in bloom

'Crispa'. It is similar to 'Anthony Waterer' but has deeply serrated leaves that are slightly twisted. 'Crispa' is a very attractive foliage plant.

'Goldflame'. This low-growing shrub offers mounds of yellowish green leaves, with reddish tips on the new growth. The foliage provides an effective canvas for the bright pink flowers. Because of its color and texture, 'Goldflame' can be a useful accent plant when mixed with other dwarf shrubs.

Spiraea japonica (Japanese spirea)

This upright, rounded, dense shrub will grow to 5 ft. tall. It has showy, pink flowers in summer and dark green foliage. There are also several worthy selections that have emerged from hybrids between Bumald spirea and Japanese spirea. As with Bumald spirea, annual early-spring pruning will encourage showy summer blooms on Japanese spirea. Hardy from Zones 4–8.

NOTABLE VARIETY

'Shirobana' ('Shibori'). This is an interesting variety, exhibiting a combination of white, pink, and rose-colored flowers. The flowers will continue sporadically into the fall. The beautifully textured leaves provide interest from spring until late fall. Mature plants will grow 2–4 ft. tall, with an equal spread.

Spiraea nipponica 'Snowmound' (Snowmound spirea)

Snowmound spirea has a dense, upright, mounded growth habit and reaches 4–5 ft. high and equally wide. Its profuse pure-white bouquets of flowers densely appear along the branches. This attractive shrub typically blooms in late spring or early summer. The clean, smooth, deep blue-green leaves are a handsome attribute during the summer months.

This species is hardy from Zones 4–7 but can be grown in Zones 3 and 8 with additional care and specific siting in a protected location. Snowmound is excellent as an informal hedge in a sunny location.

Spiraea thunbergii (Thunberg spirea)

Thunberg spirea is an old-fashioned shrub with a graceful lacy texture. It provides an impressive show in early to mid spring with masses of tiny, white flowers. The upright, cascading growth habit and small, thin leaves give this plant a wispy, broomlike appearance. The fine leaves develop a light- to medium-green color, making the plant a nice accent in the summer landscape. This species flowers on the previous season's growth, so light pruning should be done soon after the flowers have finished blooming. Selective pruning in the early spring can also be done to keep plants vigorous and productive. However, spring pruning will compromise flower output for one season.

Thunberg spirea is a very attractive shrub in a mass planting or informal hedge. Hardy from Zones 4–8.

NOTABLE VARIETY

'Ogon'. This selection has golden yellow leaves that change to chartreuse and pale green in summer. It's a very effective variety when used as an accent plant or in mass plantings. This particular variety is useful in partially shaded areas of the garden.

Spiraea × vanhoutteii (Vanhoutte spirea)

The Vanhoutte spirea is another old standard spirea. With an upright, graceful habit to 8 ft. high and 10 ft. wide, this is the largest of all the spireas described here, and it can be used as a taller informal hedge or screen. At my childhood home in Islip, New York, on Long Island, we had an informal hedge 30 ft. long by 8 ft. wide that acted as a buffer to the neighbors' yard. Each spring it would display a profusion of pure white flower clusters for a solid week before fading. Afterwards, smooth, medium-green leaves would unfurl, persisting until late fall. Even in winter this twiggy, dense shrub served as a screen.

Vanhoutte spirea requires little care and is very adaptable to soil conditions and light, although full sun is preferred. Aphids might attack the new growth and become problematic, but their damage is typically more cosmetic than life threatening. Occasional rejuvenation pruning to 12 in. from the ground in early spring will revitalize an unproductive plant and create a more compact grower. Vanhoutte spirea is hardy from Zones 3–8, but with proper siting it grows in Zone 9.

{ *Stephanandra incisa*
Cutleaf stephanandra

A graceful mounded plant, cutleaf stephanandra is an excellent deciduous shrub that can be used effectively as an informal hedge or screen. It is a multifaceted shrub, with four seasons of interest and great function in the garden. The densely arranged branches form a rounded, spreading habit, which can't be seen through even in winter. This dense habit is very attractive in winter, with conspicuous light brown stems and a cascading branching structure. The small, finely cut leaves emerge reddish bronze, before changing to medium green during the summer. The leaves eventually change to shades of yellow, orange, and red in the fall, but this transformation is not usually overwhelming. In mid- to late spring, small clusters of white flowers open, lasting for several weeks. Although a single flower cluster by itself is delicate and not particularly overpowering, en masse the clusters provide an impressive display.

© Vincent A. Simeone

Bouquets of white flowers on Vanhoutte spirea

Stephanandra is a medium-to fast-growing shrub growing 4–8 ft. tall, with an equal spread. It adapts well to many different landscape situations but really thrives in moist, well-drained, acidic soil. For best performance this shrub should be sited in full sun or partial shade.

Regular pruning is not often needed, but pruning a poorly shaped cutleaf stephanandra to 6 in. from the ground can easily rejuvenate it. Trimming or shearing into a formal shape should be avoided, as it would ruin the shrub's graceful natural growth habit. In fact, my recommendation would be to keep hedge shears as far away as possible from this elegant shrub. This plant is much more suitable as an informal planting, although its neat, uniform habit gives the appearance it is pruned often, anyway.

Stephanandra is ideal in mass plantings and as an informal hedge and, due to its dense habit, even suitable as a screening plant. It is hardy from Zones 4–7, but it will do reasonably well in Zone 8 if it receives adequate moisture and a sheltered location.

NOTABLE VARIETY

'Crispa'. This charming, compact variety has a low, creeping habit. A dwarf form, it will reach only 2–3 ft. in height, with a wider spread. It is very effective as a groundcover, in a mass planting, and as an edging plant. It can be used as a low informal hedge, as well.

Syringa spp.
Lilac

The traditional common lilac (*Syringa vulgaris*) is one of the most popular and beloved flowering shrubs in the home garden. Its masses of white, pink, purple, and violet flowers exude an intoxicating fragrance that is rivaled by few plants.

There are several reasons this species is not the ideal shrub for the home landscape, though. First, common lilac can easily outgrow a small space and will reach heights of 10–15 ft. once established. The common lilac is also prone to several pests, including leaf spots, powdery mildew, lilac borer, and scale.

It performs best in well-drained soil with a neutral (7.0) pH level but is rather adaptable. If adequate room is provided, the common lilac can function as a tall, informal screen or hedge, but I'd like to offer a few alternatives to this old garden favorite.

Today there are several species and varieties of dwarf and semi-dwarf shrubby lilacs available that exhibit amazing adaptability and function as low to medium

© Vincent A. Simeone

Stephanandra used as an informal hedge

© Vincent A. Simeone

Dense habit and finely dissected leaves of Stephanandra

informal hedges. These densely branched shrubs offer masses of pink or purple flowers, beautiful foliage, and dense growth characteristics. Admittedly, these shrub lilacs do not possess the same size, scale, and bold beauty that the common lilac exhibits, but they are delightful and valuable in their own ways. Most importantly, they are ideal as informal hedges and in small groupings.

Although common lilacs benefit from neutral-or higher-pH soils, the dwarf lilacs soon to be discussed will perform well in a wide range of soil types and pH levels. These lilacs prefer moist, well-drained soil and full sun, although they tolerate partial shade. Significant pruning is not often needed on a regular basis, but occasional selective pruning is important to keep the plants productive. Dwarf lilacs can in fact be used as formal hedges, but blooming will be compromised. Lilacs bloom on the previous season's growth, so any severe pruning in early spring will result in little or no flowering during the upcoming growing season. This is why dwarf lilacs are best when used as informal hedges, requiring little pruning. In addition, these shrubby little lilacs are excellent in mass plantings, foundation plantings, and shrub borders.

Syringa laciniata (feathered Persian lilac)

An unusual species, feathered Persian lilac has exquisite lilac-colored flowers in spring and dark green, deeply serrated leaves. This shrub can grow to 6 ft. tall and wide, with a mounded, dense growth habit. The lacy, fine-textured foliage is extremely effective in the garden long after the flowers have faded. For these

© Vincent A. Simeone

Grouping of Meyer lilacs in bud

© Vincent A. Simeone

Lilac-purple flowers of Meyer lilac

reasons, feathered Persian lilac will offer three seasons of interest in the garden. This is a very tough species, showing both cold and heat tolerance in Zones 4–8.

Syringa meyeri (Meyer lilac)

Meyer lilac forms a dense, mounded growth habit that can reach 4–8 ft. in height, with a slightly larger spread. The small, purple flowers provide a colorful display in mid- to late spring. The flowers are fragrant, although not as sweetly scented as those of common lilac. The small, glossy, green leaves provide an attractive, fine texture in the landscape. Leaves in the fall are often tinged with purple.

Meyer lilac is one of the easiest and most adaptable lilacs to grow. It prefers full sun but will tolerate partial shade. It is also pest resistant and drought tolerant and will perform well in many landscape situations. It will need a season or two to become established, but after that it will grow quickly and function well as a hedge. Hardy from Zones 3–7.

NOTABLE VARIETY

'Palibin'. This is a dwarf selection of Meyer lilac, growing only 4–5 ft. tall, with a slightly wider spread. The purple flower buds open to pink or pale purple. It is a very good lilac for the home garden.

Syringa microphylla (littleleaf lilac)

Littleleaf lilac is an old-fashioned lilac with a wide-spreading growth habit, attractive foliage, and beautiful pink flowers. An individual plant can grow 6 ft. tall and twice as wide, but not until it becomes quite old.

© Vincent A. Simeone

Littleleaf lilac in flower

© Vincent A. Simeone

Close-up of littleleaf lilac flowers

The small clusters of pink flowers offer a sweet fragrance in mid spring. These beautiful shrubs often sporadically rebloom in early fall. Another attractive feature of this fine shrub is the small, fuzzy leaves, which are soft to the touch. As littleleaf lilac matures, it forms gracefully arching branches that spill to the ground.

Littleleaf lilac is resistant to most of the common lilac problems, such as powdery mildew. It is also very adaptable to many environmental conditions but prefers moist, well-drained soil and full sun. Selective pruning to remove unproductive older branches will ensure that the plant remains healthy, productive, and somewhat compact. This lilac should not be sheared because that would ruin the graceful semi-weeping growth habit.

Littleleaf lilac is very effective as an informal hedge, mass planting, or specimen plant, as long as it is given room to spread. Hardy from Zones 4–7. This species may also perform fairly well in Zone 8 if adequate moisture is provided. In a hot, humid climate, partial shade is also beneficial.

NOTABLE VARIETY

'Superba'. This excellent variety produces masses of deep pink flowers in spring. It is a really terrific performer.

Syringa patula 'Miss Kim' (Miss Kim lilac)

The handsome Miss Kim lilac has a rounded, upright growth habit to 6 ft. tall and wide. The 3 in. clusters of purple flower buds open to fragrant, icy lavender-blue flowers in mid-to late spring. The glossy, green leaves are also quite striking, and they turn deep reddish purple in fall. 'Miss Kim' is hardy from Zones 4–7, and with additional care will grow in Zone 8.

Syringa Tinkerbelle ('Bailbelle') (Tinkerbelle lilac)

One of several introductions from the Bailey Nurseries' Fairytale series, Tinkerbelle exhibits a dwarf habit and wine-colored flower buds that in spring open to deep pink flowers with a wonderful spicy fragrance. The small, dark green leaves are the perfect backdrop to the beautiful flowers. This dwarf, floriferous shrub is ideal as informal hedges and foundation plantings for the home garden.

Other Fairytale series introductions include Prince Charming, Sugar Plum Fairy, and Thumbelina. These varieties along with Tinkerbelle are all excellent selections for cold climates, showing reliable hardiness from Zones 3–7.

Viburnum spp.
Viburnum

Viburnums are without a doubt among the most versatile and enjoyable shrub groups available for the home landscape. There are literally hundreds of species and varieties that grace our natural woodlands, as well as our cultivated landscapes. Many garden enthusiasts, growers, and horticultural experts agree that viburnums are the royalty of the woody plant kingdom.

There are several reasons such impressive accolades have been bestowed upon this exceptional group of plants. Viburnums have unmatched aesthetic value, ease of culture, and multipurpose function in the landscape. In most cases viburnums reliably offer multiple seasons of interest in the garden. They provide vibrant and sometimes fragrant flowers, colorful fruit displays, dense growth habits, and beautiful foliage. Most viburnums tend to fruit better when cross-pollinated, so planting in groupings rather than as a single specimen is recommended. Viburnums are adaptable to many climates in the United States, also. They are pest and disease resistant, drought tolerant, and become acclimated to most soils and light exposure levels. Ideally, though, viburnums thrive in moist, well-drained, acidic soil and full or partial sunlight. Viburnums also tolerate pruning very well and can easily be rejuvenated in early spring. To keep viburnums healthy and vigorous, regular selective pruning may be necessary for removing unproductive older branches. Hardiness depends on the specific species and variety and can range from Zones 3–8.

Viburnums adapt well to a variety of landscape situations. They can be used as informal or formal hedges, screenings, barrier plantings, group and mass plantings, specimens, and foundation plantings. In my garden, viburnum has earned the name "Old Reliable" because of its ability to perform famously every year. It is truly a gardener's best friend.

Viburnum × bodnantense 'Dawn' (Dawn viburnum)

The extremely fragrant Dawn viburnum displays small pink flowers at a time when most other shrubs are still dormant. I have witnessed it in bloom as early as January and as late as May in the northeastern United States. When Dawn viburnum blooms, it is usually a wake-up call that spring is just around the corner. The deep-pink flower clusters will open sporadically through the early spring when temperatures are not exceedingly cold. Besides the showy, fragrant flowers, Dawn viburnum also has deeply textured, rich green leaves during the summer months.

The upright growth habit and coarse branches make this plant a bold fixture in the landscape. Dawn viburnum can become rather awkward if left unpruned, however. I recommend that you selectively remove older stems on a regular basis. This type of maintenance pruning encourages vigorous, productive growth.

Since Dawn viburnum offers delicate, fragrant flowers early in the season, it is valued as a specimen plant and often used in shrub borders and woodland gardens. It is effective as a tall, informal hedge or screen, too, but will need occasional maintenance pruning. It is hardy from Zones 4–8, but it should be sited in a protected location in Zone 4.

Viburnum bracteatum (bracted viburnum)

Bracted viburnum is similar to arrowwood viburnum (see upcoming *Viburnum dentatum* entry) in most aspects of appearance and function. It has showy clusters of white flowers in spring and lustrous, dark green foliage. The foliage and dense habit add beautiful texture to the summer landscape. Mature plants will grow up to 10 ft. tall with an equal spread. Bracted viburnum is not quite as cold hardy as arrowwood, though, growing only from Zones 6–8.

NOTABLE VARIETY

'Emerald Luster'. This variety offers dark, lustrous leaves, creamy white flowers, and in the fall clusters of striking blackish blue fruit. It is a superior selection well worth including in the home garden.

Viburnum carlesii (Korean spicebush viburnum)

Korean spicebush viburnum has medium to dark green leaves and a dense growth habit to 6–8 ft. in height, with an equal spread. Leaves have a fuzzy texture, which often makes them look grayish green. In mid spring the deep pink flower buds open to white, snowball-like clusters of flowers, which offer a potent, spicy fragrance. Fall foliage color is reddish purple, but this can vary from year to year. Korean spicebush viburnum is an excellent deciduous shrub as an informal hedge or in mass plantings, sited where the fragrance can be enjoyed near a patio or front door. Hardy from Zones 4–8.

NOTABLE VARIETIES

'Compacta'. This compact version grows about half the size of the species, making it ideal for limited space.

'Mohawk'. This hybrid viburnum has a dense, rounded growth habit and lustrous, dark green leaves that turn brilliant shades of orange, red, and purple in autumn. The red flower buds open to white and provide a sweet, spicy fragrance in spring.

Viburnum dentatum (arrowwood viburnum)

Arrowwood viburnum is a wonderful shrub native from eastern Canada to Minnesota and south to Georgia. It received its name from the Native

© Vincent A. Simeone

Dense habit and flowers of arrowwood viburnum

© Vincent A. Simeone

Creamy white flowers of arrowwood viburnum

Americans, who used the strong, stiff branches for making shafts for their arrows. As an ornamental shrub in the home landscape, arrowwood viburnum is often overlooked, but it deserves more attention. It offers dark green, deeply serrated leaves; flat-topped, white flower clusters in spring; and clusters of deep blue or bluish black fruit in the fall. Fall foliage color varies among individual plants but may range from yellow to a brilliant red or maroon.

Arrowwood viburnum has an unmistakable presence in the landscape, with a graceful, upright growth habit reaching 10–15 ft. tall and a similar spread. For this reason it will work well as an informal tall hedge or in a grouping in the landscape. Although arrowwood viburnum needs space, it will add noticeable "bones," or structure, to the landscape. This shrub will grow well in full sun or partial shade and prefers adequate moisture and rich, well-drained soil. Arrowwood is one of the hardiest viburnums, growing from Zones 2–8. In Zone 2 it does best if sited in a sheltered location.

NOTABLE VARIETIES

In the past several years, some very good varieties of arrowwood viburnum have been developed. Here are a few exceptional selections.

Autumn Jazz ('Ralph Senior'). This is a graceful plant with yellow, orange, or burgundy fall foliage.

Blue Muffin ('Christom'). This dwarf selection has dark green, glossy leaves and clusters of brilliant blue fruit in late summer and early fall. Because it reaches only 5–7 ft. tall, with an equal width, it is ideal for the residential landscape.

'Cardinal'. A terrific selection for the autumn garden, 'Cardinal' reliably has bright red fall foliage color.

Chicago Lustre ('Synnestvedt'). This fast-growing, upright shrub has outstanding glossy foliage, making it an excellent selection for adding rich texture to the landscape.

Northern Burgundy ('Morton'). It has a very graceful growth habit and early burgundy fall foliage color.

Viburnum dilatatum (linden viburnum)

Linden viburnum is among the best viburnums for the small residential landscape. It possesses all of the ornamental virtues of many other viburnums but also offers a manageable shrubby growth habit and three seasons of interest. White, flat-topped flower clusters measuring 3–5 in. across bloom in midspring and eventually transform into clusters of bright red, cranberry-like fruit in autumn. It is one of the best viburnums available for fall fruiting interest. During the summer the rounded leaves offer a rich green color, in the fall changing to a deep red or maroon.

The growth habit of linden viburnum is upright and dense, reaching 8 ft. tall, with a similar spread. This shrub is suitable in a foundation planting, grouping, mass planting, woodland garden, or as a small specimen plant mixed in a perennial border. It grows best in hardiness Zones 5–7, but in the right landscape situation, it will grow in Zones 4 or 8.

Cranberrybush viburnum in summer

NOTABLE VARIETIES

'Asian Beauty'. The large, dark green leaves and bright red fruit offer a handsome contrast.

'Catskill'. Here's a compact selection, reaching 5–6 ft. in height.

'Erie'. This large-flowering selection, with flowers up to 6 in. across, is also an excellent fruit bearer.

'Michael Dodge'. An unusual selection with yellow fruit, it makes a very nice accent plant for the gardener who wants to introduce something new and bold into the garden.

Viburnum opulus and *V. trilobum* (cranberrybush viburnums)

The American cranberrybush viburnum (*Viburnum trilobum*) and the European cranberrybush viburnum

(*V. opulus*) are well known in gardens around the world. As the names suggest, they possess bright red, cranberry-like fruit, which ripens in late summer and early fall. The fruit tends to have a translucent glow when ripe and will often persist through part of the winter. American cranberrybush viburnum has edible fruit that is sometimes used for jams and jellies. Both species of cranberrybush viburnum tend to set fruit more reliably when planted in groups, where they will cross-pollinate.

White, rounded or flat-topped flower clusters emerge en masse in spring. The distinct leaf has three lobes, making it look like a maple leaf. Foliage coloration in the autumn can range from yellow to deep red or maroon.

These dense, upright shrubs can grow to 12 ft. in height, with a similar spread. For best flowering and fruit display, the shrubs should be grown in full sun or partial shade. Cranberrybush viburnum prefers moist, well-drained soil but is very adaptable.

Cranberrybush viburnum is an excellent choice for a woodland setting, mass planting, background, or screen. One effective way to distinguish these two species from other shrubs is to locate the suction-cup–like glands along the leaf stem. American cranberrybush is best suited to grow from Zones 2–7, whereas its European counterpart grows from Zones 3–8.

NOTABLE AMERICAN CRANBERRYBUSH VARIETIES

'Compactum'. This low-growing form has an excellent, dense growth habit. Its flowers and fruit are also very showy. Like the compact variety of the European Cranberrybush viburnum (also named 'Compactum'),

this selection is very effective in a small garden or in an area with limited space. It's also effective in combination with perennials.

'Wentworth'. It was selected in the early 1900s for its larger, edible fruit, which ripens in stages, starting with a yellow-red coloration and eventually aging to bright red.

NOTABLE EUROPEAN CRANBERRYBUSH VARIETIES

'Compactum'. This very fine variety grows to only 6 ft. high and wide. It is an extremely dense plant and has an extraordinary fruit display in the fall. 'Compactum' is an excellent choice for the home garden, as it is more suitable for the landscape with limited space. It is ideal in mass plantings, small groupings, and foundation plantings. You will be the envy of the neighborhood!

'Nanum'. A low-growing selection, 'Nanum' becomes 2–3 ft. tall, with a similar spread. This shrub is not known as being particularly heavily flowering or fruiting, but it is grown because it offers a dense growth habit and nice foliage. 'Nanum' is perfect as a low hedge, edging plant or foundation planting.

'Notcutt'. This variety features large white flowers and striking red fruit, plus excellent maroon fall color. This selection has a reputation as a good performer and an extremely showy plant in the landscape.

Viburnum plicatum var. *tomentosum* (doublefile viburnum)

One of the most popular and versatile viburnums for the home garden, doublefile viburnum came by its name from the double row of white flowers that line up along the stems like soldiers at attention. Flat, pure white flower clusters that resemble lace cap hydrangea flowers emerge in midspring and transform into deep red fruit in mid- to late summer. This species is one of the first viburnums in the summer to display colorful fruit, which various species of birds will enjoy. The deeply ridged leaves provide wonderful texture during the summer and turn red or maroon in fall.

Doublefile viburnum has a uniquely graceful growth habit, with the lateral branches typically growing in a horizontal arrangement. Mature plants can reach 8–10 ft. tall with a slightly wider spread. Once established, this shrub will make an impressive specimen and become the focal point of the garden. A small grouping strategically placed in the garden will also act as a rather interesting screen. It does best from Zones 5–7, but it will grow in Zone 8 with adequate moisture and appropriate siting in a protected location.

© Vincent A. Simeone

Doublefile viburnum in flower

NOTABLE VARIETIES

'Mariesii'. This excellent, reliable performer has large, white flowers, beautiful red fruit, and superior red fall color. Its very distinct horizontal branching habit distinguishes this plant from all of the others in the garden.

'Molly Schroeder'. This new selection displays pink flowers in spring, and if growing conditions permit, it may sporadically rebloom in the fall, providing another show.

'Shasta'. This is a wide-spreading selection, reaching 7 ft. tall and 12 ft. wide. It has large, showy flowers, bright red fruit, and purple to maroon fall foliage coloration. A garden gem!

'Shoshoni'. This variety offers a semi-dwarf habit growing 5–6 ft. in height with a slightly wider spread, making it appropriate for the small landscape, for a perennial border, or as a foundation planting.

'Summer Snowflake'. This is a truly dwarf plant, reaching only 6 ft. tall, making it smaller than most doublefile viburnum varieties. It flowers heavily for the first few weeks and then sporadically throughout the rest of the summer season and into the autumn. This very semi-dwarf plant also offers showy red fruit.

Viburnum plicatum (Japanese snowball viburnum)

While the doublefile viburnum (*Viburnum plicatum* var. *tomentosum*) is undoubtedly a popular plant, the

Japanese snowball viburnum (the species of which the doublefile viburnum is a variety) can also be a beautiful addition to the garden. It is similar to the doublefile viburnum, but its flowers develop into rounded, pompoms similar to a mophead hydrangea, but smaller. The growth habit of Japanese snowball tends to be more upright and less spreading than the doublefile viburnum.

NOTABLE VARIETIES
'Grandiflorum'. An attractive shrub with a noticeably horizontal branching habit, it shows off large white flowers and beautiful green foliage.

'Kern's Pink'. The flowers bloom in varying degrees of solid pink or white with pink tones. The spring foliage is tinged red.

'Mary Milton'. This unique shrub offers attractive medium pink flowers that are often accompanied by a combination of pale pink flowers as well. The new, pleated foliage in the spring is tinged with red, similar to that of 'Kern's Pink'.

Viburnum sieboldii (Siebold viburnum)
Several *Viburnum* species grow into large shrubs or small trees. One of the most popular is the Siebold viburnum. This large-scale plant adds a bold texture to the landscape with its large, oblong leaves, which are a dark, lustrous green with very pronounced veins. Creamy white, flat-topped flower clusters emerge at the end of each branch in spring. The glossy, bright red fruit clusters ripen in late summer or early fall and provide enjoyable meals for birds. The overall growth pattern is upright and dense at youth and eventually reaches 15–20 ft. high. Foliage can turn reddish purple in fall.

Siebold viburnum is an adaptable plant but prefers well-drained, moist soil and full sun or partial shade. It is an excellent small specimen tree for a home garden and is also effective in mass plantings and as a screen. Hardy from Zones 4–8. Also deer resistant.

Weigela florida
Old-fashioned weigela
Like viburnum and spirea, old-fashioned weigela is a longtime favorite that is once again gaining in popularity. This easy-to-grow, floriferous shrub produces masses of small, pink, trumpet-like flowers in midspring and often sporadically through the growing season. Weigela typically grows 6 ft. high, with an equal or greater spread, and has gracefully arching branches that sweep down to the ground. The medium-green leaves provide a nice backdrop to the showy flowers.

Weigela, not a particularly finicky garden inhabitant, will adapt to varying soils and light exposure levels. For best results, plant weigela in full sun and moist, well-drained garden soil. Pruning can be done several ways, depending on the desired outcome. To keep plants healthy and productive, occasional selective pruning to remove older, mature stems should be done in early spring. If a shrub requires such spring pruning, some flowering will be sacrificed, but the following year the plant will produce masses of blooms. If an old-fashioned weigela is too overgrown or leggy, pruning it down to 12 in. will rejuvenate it. If shaping or simple maintenance pruning is needed, wait until after the shrub has finished flowering.

Weigela is a multipurpose flowering shrub that can be used much like forsythia and spirea. It is very effective in mass plantings, groups, informal hedges, and foundation plantings. If maintained properly, this fine shrub develops a beautiful arching habit that will be admired throughout the year. Hardy from Zones 5–8 and, with adequate moisture and specific siting in a partially shaded location in the garden, possibly Zone 9. The varieties with maroon-colored leaves, such as Wine and Roses, will likely hold their leaf color better in cooler climates.

NOTABLE VARIETIES

The more recent varieties described here are excellent additions to the residential landscape, displaying improved foliage and flowers and compact growth habits.

'Minuet'. This densely compact shrub grows 2–3 ft. tall and has deep red flowers. The dark green leaves are tinged with purple for a nice foliage effect.

'Red Prince'. An upright-growing shrub, it features cherry red blossoms that will continue sporadically through early summer.

'Rubidor'. The combination of bright yellow foliage and deep rosy pink flowers make this plant the neon sign of the garden. It is useful as an accent plant in a partially shaded area of the garden. The combination of flowers and foliage can be quite an overwhelming contrast, so using this plant as a cutback shrub will enhance foliage color while reducing flower production.

'Variegata'. This is a popular garden variety, with its pale-yellow leaf edges and deep rose–colored flowers. This makes for a very attractive accent plant in the garden. The foliage accent can be boosted by using 'Variegata' as a cutback shrub.

Wine and Roses ('Alexandra'). This delightful variety has deep burgundy leaves, similar in color to a fine red wine, and rosy pink flowers that look like a bouquet of roses. The contrast between leaves and flowers is outstanding. Wine and Roses can also be effectively used as a cutback shrub, which will highlight its beautiful-colored foliage.

Site Selection and Plant Care

A well-designed garden is both functional and aesthetically pleasing. By properly assessing growing conditions and understanding the needs of specific trees and shrubs, the gardener can make sound decisions on plants that will thrive in the garden. In addition, knowing the cultural requirements of your woody plant candidates is vital to choosing ones that will succeed. Correct planting procedures, adequate soil moisture, pruning, and fertilization are all important aspects of gardening to consider. Proper care will result in healthy, productive, and beautiful plants that will offer years of enjoyment.

SITE ASSESSMENT

Before selecting evergreens or deciduous shrubs, it is essential that gardeners understand some key factors about the landscape, such as soil type, light exposure, and climate changes. With proper research to determine the appropriate garden areas for your favorite plants, many gardening miscues will be avoided.

SOIL

Garden soil can vary greatly in many areas of the United States. It is essential that you test your soil pH and determine your soil's texture before planting. Soil texture and composition can range from heavy, clay soil to well-drained, loamy soil to light, sandy soil. These basic classes represent the ability of different types of soil to retain moisture and nutrients. Though most of the trees discussed in this book perform best in moist but well-drained soil, some trees and shrubs need special conditions.

Soil pH—its relative acidity or alkalinity—is also an important factor. Certain plant groups, such as rhododendrons, prefer acidic soil, whereas others, such as lilac, prefer or adapt to neutral or alkaline soil. However, the majority of the plants presented in this book are adaptable to a variety of soil pH levels. Soil pH is measured on a scale from 1 to 14, in which 7.0 is neutral. Soil pH below 7.0 is considered acidic; soil pH above 7.0 is alkaline. A soil pH meter or test kit, which can be purchased in a local garden center or nursery, will allow you to determine the pH of your garden soil. In addition, soil samples can be brought to your local extension service for testing. Soil testing may also provide valuable diagnostic and treatment information for existing plants that are not performing well in your landscape.

Soil pH can be raised or lowered by adding products to the soil. For example, garden lime (calcium carbonate) can be added to raise the pH, whereas aluminum sulfate will acidify soil. Such natural products as manure and compost also generally acidify the soil. Soil pH should be altered gradually, over an extended period of time, however, so only a limited amount of such materials should be added to soil at one time.

LIGHT EXPOSURE

Light exposure, how sunny or shady your garden is, plays an important role in the success of your trees and shrubs. There are three basic types of natural light in the garden: full sun, partial shade, or shade—with variations of each. Certain plants prefer full sun, whereas others need the protection provided by taller trees overhead. For example, rhododendrons prefer partial shade while junipers thrive in full sun. Plants such as arborvitae, pine, spruce and fir are rather adaptable to variations in light exposures.

You can determine the types of light exposure in various parts of your garden by closely monitoring the sunlight from hour to hour. This is generally best done around June 21, the summer solstice, when the sun is at its highest point. Garden areas that receive at least five or six hours of direct sunlight a day are considered full sun sites. Fewer hours than that are considered different degrees of shade, from light to dense. Partial shade is where plants receive about four hours or less of sun, either direct or indirect, per day. In partial shade, if the plants do get direct sun, it is usually early or late in the day, often coming in at a lower angle under the canopy of tall trees. Full or dense shade refers to an area of the garden in no direct sun.

WIND EXPOSURE

It is important to know the amount of wind that different areas of your garden experience. Certain plants will tolerate wind better than others. High wind exposure is often found in coastal areas, exposed mountainsides, or open prairies. In such cases, only a select group of plants that will tolerate these exposed conditions can be chosen. For example, rhododendron and falsecypress are not particularly tolerant of windy sites, but junipers are. Of course, other factors that effect wind exposure and its intensity are land topography; surrounding barriers such as fences, buildings, and large tree canopy; and time of year. In the winter months wind exposure can be especially harsh and damaging because leafless deciduous plants don't provide foliage cover.

SELECTING THE RIGHT PLANT FOR THE APPROPRIATE LOCATION

Once you have determined the makeup of your garden's soil, light exposure, wind conditions, and any other physical characteristics, another set of issues concerning plant selection must be addressed. You must determine what you are hoping to accomplish when using a tree or shrub in the garden. What is the desired function? Do you need a mass planting for spring color? A grouping of shrubs to screen an unsightly view? Or a low planting near the foundation of your house to add interest?

What colors and textures are you interested in introducing into the garden? How will these new plants look with other existing plant material? And, most important, will the trees and shrubs you have chosen outgrow the spaces you have selected for them? Putting a woody plant in too small of a site will only lead to problems in the future.

One suggestion for gardeners willing to invest the time is to create a checklist to identify your desired goals and needs; this should accompany a list of existing environmental conditions. These will help to shape a concise list of potential screening plants. For example, a homeowner has decided that a tall, informal screen is needed to reduce wind and screen an unsightly village road. This particular garden setting is in full sun, has sandy soils and is located near an exposed, seashore environment. All of these factors will greatly reduce what can be grown in this landscape environment. The best choices in this situation would be *Juniperus virginiana* (eastern red cedar), *Ilex glabra* (inkberry holly), or *Berberis julianae* (wintergreen barberry).

Answering a few simple questions and taking some time to properly plan your garden planting project will most certainly ensure success.

PROPER PLANTING

It is imperative that proper planting techniques be applied when planting or transplanting trees and shrubs. It is not enough simply to dig a hole and place soil around the root-ball of the plant. Special care must be taken in preparing the planting site. This planning will ensure that your valuable plants thrive in their new setting. It is also very important to understand that generally, the larger the tree or shrub, the longer it takes to become established in its new home, due to transplant shock.

Several important steps should be followed when planting woody plants. The best time to plant a shrub or tree is in spring or fall while the air temperature is cool and the soil is moist. Exact timing depends on the specific climate where you live and the species of tree being planted. No planting should be done during the extremes of summer or winter.

Again, you have selected your plant with consideration of the garden soil's characteristics. Specific location is important, too, depending on the tree's purpose in your garden's overall scheme and its requirements for light and protection from the elements. Of course, be sure to site your flowering tree in an area of the garden where it will have plenty of room to grow.

Now the planting hole can be prepared. The size of the hole depends on the size of the root-ball. When a tree or shrub is purchased from a plant nursery, it is typically growing as a balled-and-burlapped (B&B) plant or in a container. Burlap is a rough cloth material that covers and supports the roots and soil of a plant, perhaps with help from rope, wire, or plastic, until future planting in another location. Containers can range in size and type but are often made of plastic. In either case, the planting hole should be at least three times as wide as the diameter of the root-ball. This will allow the roots to become established in loose, fluffy soil.

It is very important that your tree or shrub be placed at the proper depth in the soil. Trees and shrubs that are planted too deeply are doomed to fail; they

How to plant an Evergreen Properly

1. Place the root-ball on firm undisturbed soil at or slightly above ground level.

2. When the tree is safely placed in the ground, carefully cut and remove the top one-third of any wire baskets, removing all nylon ropes and burlap that may be attached to the root-ball.

3. Backfill the planting hole with soil.

4. Top dress with 1-2 in. of mulch or wood chips.

5. The top of the root-ball should be flush or slightly above grade to expose the root flare.

6. Water regularly after planting.

often decline slowly, but they will eventually succumb. When planting your new tree or shrub, the top of the root-ball should be even with or slightly above the soil level. With a B&B plant, peel back the top of the burlap to check this; the rest of the burlap should stay in place during these early stages of the planting procedure to help hold the root-ball together. As a general rule I recommend placing the tree or shrub so that the top of the root-ball is slightly above (about 1 in). the soil line.

Be sure the root-ball soil itself isn't built up too high on the trunk. Trees have what is known as a root flare, the bulging area where the trunk meets the soil (see illustration). Most trees, with few exceptions, have a root flare, which is usually most evident in trees with trunks 2 in. or thicker. (Although shrubs do not often have a visible root flare, all of these procedures basically apply.) If the root flare of your new purchase is not visible, it could be an indication that soil is covering it. Gently remove soil from the top of the root-ball to expose the root flare. Once you've done this, situating the tree in the planting hole will be easy. Make sure that the tree does not settle too low in the planting hole, which might allow the flare to become covered again when you fill in the hole or even naturally.

These root flare tips can also help you with an established tree or shrub that is planted too deeply or that has had soil accumulate against its trunk over time. Again, gently remove any soil from the trunk to expose the root flare, if it has one.

Once you've got the root-ball and tree sitting at the right height in the hole, remove as much rope, plastic, wire, burlap, and so on as possible from the planting

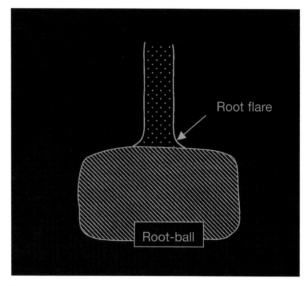

hole to ensure proper growth. It is very important, though, not to break or damage the root-ball in any way. If removal of all of the burlap or wire basket is not possible without damaging the root-ball, carefully remove this material from just the top third to half of the root-ball.

At the time of purchase, make sure to ask your nursery professional which type of burlap is on your plant's root-ball. Some burlap may be treated with a product that inhibits it from decaying, as often indicated by a green coloration. Treated burlap, if left in the planting hole, may remain relatively intact for many years and interfere with root growth. Therefore, as much treated burlap as possible should be cut out of the planting hole and discarded. Untreated burlap, on the other hand, will naturally break down. Although as much of it as possible should be removed from the planting hole, leaving some in is not much of a concern because it will rot fairly quickly underground and not block the roots.

Container-grown shrubs and trees are handled quite differently by the nursery from those that are balled and burlapped. Shrubs and trees growing in a container has very often become pot-bound, meaning that there is a large volume of roots that fill the container. As growing roots reach the side of the pot, they have nowhere to go but around and around, forming a thick mesh. When you pull your new tree and its root-ball from the container, you may need to tease out such a fibrous web of roots carefully, or gently slice it apart with a knife to open it up. This will encourage the roots to grow out into the planting site soil.

Regardless of whether your new plant arrives balled and burlapped or in a container, the planting procedure is similar (see illustration of proper planting techniques of an evergreen tree). Once the planting hole has been prepared and the tree is straight and set at the appropriate depth, the soil can be backfilled into the planting hole and lightly tamped. This will reduce large air pockets and settling of soil when watering is done. The planting hole should be free from large rocks, old roots, and other debris, which should be discarded. Excess soil should also be removed once the planting hole has been filled. If the surrounding soil is poor (rocky, heavy clay, etc.) it would be beneficial to incorporate organic matter such as well aged compost (composted leaves or manure) to the planting hole. After the planting process is complete the tree or shrub should be watered thoroughly and slowly, so that the entire planting area is evenly moist. If settling occurs causing the tree to become crooked in the planting hole, additional steps such as staking may be needed. A thin layer of mulch covering the soil around the root-ball will reduce soil moisture fluctuations and weed growth. A newly planted tree or shrub should be watered regularly in the growing season for at least two growing seasons to ensure its establishment.

CARING FOR EVERGREENS

In addition to their aesthetic value and function in the landscape, evergreens also have unique cultural requirements that need special consideration. Typically, evergreens require different care than deciduous plant material, and additional cultural practices are often needed to satisfy their specific growing requirements. This is especially true in regions of the country where harsh conditions and fluctuations in climate occur. Extremes in heat or cold, hot and dry, cold and wet, etc. can all effect how well evergreens perform in the landscape. Generally evergreens prefer moderated conditions without large fluctuations in temperature, rainfall, etc. As a general rule, evergreens require even soil moisture and are more likely to be damaged by cold winter temperatures and desiccating winds than deciduous plants. Although deciduous trees and shrubs can be affected by heat and drought stress during the summer months along with evergreens, they are not usually susceptible to the same winter damage, since they shed their leaves in the fall. Even though evergreens are essentially dormant in winter, they may still experience water loss through their leaves on warm, sunny days. The combination of the harsh winter temperatures and drying winds can cause winter burn. For this reason, if in a region where extended periods of severe cold temperatures are experienced, you need to take extra care to protect your plants.

Winter desiccation can be a problem with evergreens even if there is adequate moisture in the soil. During the winter, cold or frozen soil makes it difficult for roots to absorb and translocate water to leaves and stems. This causes the leaves to dry up, and the surface of the leaf will have a burned appearance. When evergreen leaves wilt in the winter, it is a protective measure to conserve water and reduce water loss through the leaves.

To reduce winter stress by reducing water loss and leaf damage, anti-desiccants can be applied to evergreen trees and shrubs. Anti-desiccants form a protective waxy layer on the surface of the leaf, this is especially beneficial to broadleaf evergreens. Application of an anti-desiccant is usually done during the late fall or winter months, although it should not be applied when air temperatures are below freezing. It is important to consult your local county extension agent, garden center, or nursery professional before using such a product. Also, it is imperative that you first read the directions on the label. Among the important guidelines you'll get from these sources is that anti-desiccants should be applied only to certain species and varieties of plants. For example, if an anti-dessicant were applied to a plant with blue foliage, such as Colorado blue spruce, the needles would turn green.

Some products, by the way, can also be used in the summer to reduce drought and heat stress. As mentioned earlier, evergreens can also be vulnerable in regions that experience hot, dry summers. Heat, drought, and humidity can create challenges for your evergreen plant material.

There are other ways besides anti-desiccants to protect plants in winter. Wrapping plants with burlap and twine will protect them from wind, ice, and snow. Heavy snow loads can break or bend branches and cause severe physical damage. By tying branches close together on certain plants, extra support is given to the entire plant to withstand the harsh elements of winter. This is also dependent on the species of tree or shrub in question. For example, American arborvitae (*Thuja occidentalis*) is much more susceptible to breakage than western arborvitae (*T. plicata*).

MULCHING AND FERTILIZING

Stressed plants are more vulnerable than other plants and may be severely damaged or killed by the severe extremes of winter or summer. Mulching trees and shrubs with 1–2 in. of wood chips, pine straw, shredded leaves, or compost will protect their roots during the harsh conditions of summer and winter by helping to moderate soil temperature.

New plantings should be given six months to a year to become established before being put on a regular fertilizer program. Before any fertilizer is applied, a soil test should be taken to evaluate the specific needs of the soil. Soil samples can be taken to your local county extension agent for testing. If fertilizer is necessary or desired, it should be applied between fall and early spring, while plants are dormant. Evergreens can be fertilized with a balanced fertilizer, such as 10-6-4 or 5-10-5. There are many fertilizer formulations on the market, so check with your local garden center or nursery professional for proper selection of a fertilizer for your specific situation.

In addition to the fertilizers mentioned, natural products such as mulch and compost also act as fertilizer for plants. Organic compost products will improve the soil, provide natural fertilizer, and improve the water-holding capacity of the soil. Compost is organic material, such as leaves or manure, that has been aged to create humus. Humus is a brown or black organic substance consisting of partially or wholly decayed vegetable or animal matter; it provides nutrients for plants and increases the ability of soil to retain water. Humus is an excellent form of natural fertilizer that plants can readily use.

Organic fertilizer is one of the best substances for fertilizing plants because it is environmentally friendly and much less likely to damage plants, unlike conventional chemical fertilizers, which can damage plants directly, or more gradually through overfertilized soil, if applied too heavily.

After planting a new tree, a circle of mulch on the surface of the soil, at least as wide as the planting hole, will greatly benefit your plant. Even an established tree will benefit from a thin, circular layer of mulch. Mulching frequency depends on how fast the material decomposes. As previously mentioned, the best mulch products are natural organic materials, such as shredded leaves, wood chips, pine straw, and compost.

WATERING

Proper watering practices are crucial to the survival and success of evergreens in your garden. Stressed plants that receive too much or too little water are typically more vulnerable to pests and disease and in severe cases death can occur. In the case of new planting, regular watering is important during spring, summer and fall for the first two years after installation. In the case of established plantings, supplemental irrigation during periods of drought is also important. Whether newly installed or established, evergreens should also receive a thorough, deep watering prior to going dormant with the onset of the cold winter temperatures. Generally in climates where supplemental irrigation is required and in periods of drought, longer, infrequent watering is preferred over short, frequent watering. Specific watering amounts depend of soil types, species of the plant, and several other factors. For example, during hot, dry summers when plants are not receiving enough natural rainfall, watering trees and shrubs for two to four hours, once or twice a week will provide a deep watering. With new plantings that have not established, more frequent watering in times of drought may be necessary. Deep watering will encourage the establishment of a healthy root system. In contrast, short, frequent waterings—such as watering five times a week for thirty minutes each time—will only moisten the surface of the soil, creating plants with shallow, vulnerable root systems. Very often this type of watering will waste valuable water since much of the water will evaporate in hot weather or be absorbed by turf instead of penetrating the surface of the soil to the tree roots. Watering frequency is very dependent on climate, soil types, and plant species. Heavy, clay loam soils or rich, organic soils tend to dry out less often than sandy soils. For more information, consult with your local water authority and cooperative extension agent on water restrictions and watering recommendations in your area.

INTEGRATED PEST MANAGEMENT

Integrated pest management, or IPM, is a very important component of a garden maintenance program. The main goals of IPM are to develop a sustainable landscape by managing pests effectively and efficiently and to help people to use methods that minimize environmental, health, and economic risks. A successful IPM program incorporates garden monitoring and many forms of pest control, such as biological, cultural, physical or mechanical, and chemical controls, as well as proper plant selection.

The most important factor associated with IPM is monitoring the landscape. Gardeners must regularly scout the landscape to observe the types and quantities of pests that might be present. If a low pest population is observed, no action may be necessary. Once a pest has crossed a certain population or damage threshold or caused some other concern, it may be necessary to take action. One excellent way to monitor pest populations is through pest traps, which are usually attractive to insects because of color or scent.

Through systematic monitoring of traps, the gardener can pinpoint when a pest has arrived in the garden, how the population is growing, and then decide whether control is justified.

Biological controls have become very popular because they control pests with little or no need for pesticides. Biological controls are beneficial insects and other organisms that reduce pest numbers, perhaps by preying on them or infecting them with a pest-specific disease. Although many beneficial organisms are common insects we can easily recognize, others are microscopic and harder to detect. One good example of an effective beneficial insect that reduces harmful pest populations is the ladybug, which eats aphids. Other beneficial insects include *Encarsia* (a wasp that preys on whitefly), *Cryptolaemus* (mealybug killers), and BT (*Bacillus thuringiensis*), a beneficial bacterium that preys on caterpillars. Several garden supply companies offer beneficial insects for release into the garden.

Physical and mechanical controls are very similar and also require no chemicals. You can physically remove or kill harmful pests simply by taking action. For example, scale can be wiped off plants very easily with just a cloth and rubbing alcohol. Although this physical method is very time consuming, it is also very safe to the plant and the environment. Mechanical control is similar, but it usually involves some type of machinery. Using a pole pruner or lopping shears to remove invasive vines that are strangling your valuable evergreens is a good example of this. Or harmful beetles can live and breed in brush piles and other wood debris. A wood chipper eliminates brush and reduces the beetle population.

Cultural practices, a very important component of IPM, are usually related to reducing disease or insect problems through sanitation. The main goal of using sound cultural practices is to create optimal environmental conditions for plants and to reduce plant stress. This will result in the reduced likelihood of plants being vulnerable to pest problems. In essence, healthy, thriving plants are generally less susceptible to diseases and insects.

One facet of IPM that is very effective is to plant genetically superior or pest-resistant plants to start with. New varieties of landscape plants and agricultural crops are being developed on a regular basis. These plants are bred for pest resistance, drought tolerance, and improved aesthetic value. Many experts feel that using superior plants in appropriate locations will significantly reduce pest problems and the need for pesticides. Universities have plant evaluation and selection programs to evaluate plants for such purposes. The results of these programs filter down to farmers, nurserymen, retailers, and, eventually, homeowners.

Chemical controls, such as pesticides, are usually considered a last resort in an effective IPM program, which encourages alternatives to pesticides whenever possible. If it seems that all other reasonable means of control have failed and there is no other choice, though, chemical control can be considered. Be sure to contact your local agricultural extension service or horticultural professional for advice. If a pesticide is needed to control a pest, the environmentally safest, least-harmful product should be considered first. Good examples of lower-toxicity pesticides are horticultural oils and soaps, which break down quickly in the environment, with few lingering residual effects. Before applying any pesticide, it is imperative to read the label carefully.

With proper monitoring and implementation of sound pest management practices, landscapes can be maintained more efficiently and effectively. This creates a productive, safe, and aesthetically pleasing environment for all to enjoy.

PRUNING

Proper pruning techniques are important for maintaining healthy, beautiful shrubs and trees. An ongoing pruning schedule will result in vigorous, productive plants that maximize growth. This doesn't mean that your evergreens need to be pruned constantly; rather, they should be monitored and pruned as needed to accomplish the desired goal or function they were intended for.

Several factors must be considered before pruning an evergreen. The two most important are to determine the type of evergreen you are pruning and its intended purpose. For example, the purpose might be to create a formal hedge, but if the wrong species is chosen, the outcome may be disappointing. Certain species of evergreens can be pruned more often or more severely than others and are thus more suitable for a formal hedge. Yews, hollies, and mountain laurel can be rejuvenated with severe pruning if done at the right time of the year (early spring), and they will respond positively, provided they are healthy and not stressed. Such plants as junipers, arborvitaes, falsecypresses, and most pines cannot be pruned so severely that all or most of their green leaves are removed all at once. This type of pruning would likely result in seriously disfiguring or killing your plants.

In most landscape situations where hedges or screens are desirable, maintenance pruning or shearing is recommended. Shearing to create a formal hedge or more maintained look can be accomplished easily with a regular pruning program. Whether you are creating a formal or an informal hedge, yews, hollies, boxwoods, and euonymus are just a few examples of shrubs that respond well to shearing. The main goal with shearing shrubs is not to take off too much growth at one time but rather to remove smaller amounts of growth more often to maintain a certain shape or size. For example, if you have a yew hedge that you want to maintain at 6 ft. tall, pruning several times a growing season to that desired height would accomplish that goal. However, if you have a grouping of Leyland cypress that you want to reach 30 ft., little or no pruning is necessary. In the case of flowering evergreen shrubs or conifers such as spruce, fir, and falsecypress, a more natural, informal look is recommended.

Pruning dead, diseased, or broken branches can be done at any time of the year with little negative impact to the plant. Remember that pruning late in the season can stimulate the plant to grow, leaving the new, fleshy growth vulnerable to frost and the cold temperatures of autumn.

In reference to deciduous shrubs that are being used as a hedge or screen, similar rules apply. If an informal hedge is desired, occasional selective pruning to remove older, less productive stems is recommended while the plant is dormant in late winter or early spring. For example, an established forsythia hedge can and should be maintained with selective pruning. Every two to three years look for old, thick, damaged, or unproductive stems and prune them near the ground leaving the younger, vigorous stems to grow. However, this should only done as needed since some plants may not need this frequency of selective pruning. This will keep plants healthy and productive.

If your hedge is too overgrown, not flowering well, or out of shape, a more severe rejuvenation pruning may be needed. This type of pruning requires gardeners to prune plants down to 6–12 in. from the ground while plants are dormant. The result will be a flush of new, vibrant growth that will develop into a new informal hedge. However, remember that shrubs such as forsythia, viburnum, and weigela all bloom on the previous season's growth, so the first year of bloom after severe pruning will be sacrificed. If severe pruning is not needed, lightly pruning shrubs right after flowering will not sacrifice next year's blooms and still allow gardeners to maintain and shape healthy plants. In most cases I do not recommend shearing or shaping flowering deciduous shrubs but rather recommend maintaining these plants as informal hedges.

Proper pruning tools are essential for maintaining healthy and productive trees and shrubs that will produce lush growth and showy flowers and fruit.

Though there are many valuable tools that a gardener may use from time to time, none are more important than hand pruning shears, lopping shears, and a handsaw.

A good hand pruner is one of the most important tools used to maintain healthy trees and shrubs. There are several types of hand-held pruners, but a bypass type is the most appropriate. This type of pruner works like scissors, one blade passing by the other, and is effective because it cleanly cuts branches without crushing them.

Lopping shears are long-handled pruners that allow more leverage for cutting larger branches than hand pruners. The handles can be made of metal, wood, or fiberglass, and the blades should also be of the bypass type.

A handheld pruning saw is used to prune large branches that are typically too large for lopping shears to cut. A sharp, thin saw will enable a gardener to effectively reach tight areas within a large mass of branches.

Hedge shears, whether motorized or manually operated, should be used with discretion. Their purpose is to remove small amounts of growth from the tips of plants, typically to maintain shrubs in a more manicured manner.

All tools must be kept sharp, clean, and well oiled. Regular maintenance should be performed to ensure proper tool effectiveness. Failure to maintain tools properly may result in unnecessary damage to your trees and shrubs, such as jagged or sloppy cuts.

Landscaping with Screening Plants

Although it is important to know the aesthetic value and growing requirements of both evergreen and deciduous plant material in the landscape, it is equally crucial to understand their functions in the garden. In addition to ornamental value, woody plants provide structure and year-round interest in the landscape. Although the primary function of screening plants is to provide aesthetic value, security and privacy to your home, screening plants can also reduce roadway noise, glare, wind, and extreme temperatures.

Landscape design techniques are potentially very complex and can be a challenging part of gardening. Landscape design is essential, though, to the success of your living screens. A poorly planned landscape is doomed for failure. One of the most common miscues of gardeners, for instance, is failing to supply a plant with enough space to grow. It is easy to underestimate the overall spread of the tree or shrub. Be sure to carefully select the appropriate site for every plant. A tree or shrub that is misplaced may have to be pruned regularly to control their size, and then they often become disfigured and unproductive over time.

A second siting miscue is simply planting trees and shrubs with no real plan or purpose. Placing a few trees and shrubs randomly through the garden can create a confusing, distracting landscape of limited effectiveness. Proper design techniques can create continuity and excitement in the home landscape.

Following are some tips on how to incorporate plants in the landscape so they are effective as screens and hedges and can provide privacy and security from the outside world.

CONTINUITY

It is very important that your landscape have continuity and repetition. Groupings or mass plantings of one type or a few types of plants can be highly effective. When planting your screening or hedge, it is highly recommended that you choose one or two compatible plants for groupings or mass plantings. Plantings with too many different plants could be confusing and disorderly.

DESIGN PATTERN

There are two basic types of planting approaches for screens or hedges: formal and informal. With a formal planting you typically plant several trees or shrubs, all of one type, in a straight line or at right angles (see illustrations). A formal planting is also created by shearing or regularly pruning plants to create a tight, dense

Formal screen or hedge

3D view of formal screen or hedge

Informal hedge or Screen

3-D View of informal hedge or screen

mass of growth. This neat, manicured, and organized appearance is known as formal.

An informal planting is created and maintained quite differently. It is much looser and more natural in appearance. It can be laid out in a random, staggered pattern or in a straight line, but the distiquishing characteristic is how it is pruned (see the lower illustrations). Informal plantings are left to grow with modest or infrequent pruning allowing them to display their natural growth habit. This allows a much more open or graceful effect to the growth of the plants, while they still function as a screen. This type of hedge tends to create a healthier, more productive planting over time.

BERMING

Berming is the common practice of mounding soil to create small, sweeping hills. The main purposes of a berm are to create interest while increasing the potential for privacy in the landscape. Varying height levels gives character to a landscape that would otherwise be flat and rather mundane. Berms enhance the effectiveness of plant materials in screening undesirable views and creating a noise and wind barrier. Berms are also effective where retaining walls are not necessary.

However, a gardener should take special care to ensure that every berm is in scale with the rest of the landscape. The size of a berm will be determined by its surroundings and the ultimate size of the plants on them. In general, a berm should be at least five to six times as long as it is high, and it should gradually spill into the garden. As a natural element in the landscape, a berm should be visually compatible and harmonious with its surroundings. One way to enhance the natural appearance of a berm is to vary its slopes by applying gradual transitions in elevation. The slope ratios in most cases should be between 5:1 and 7:1, or five to seven times wider than high to ensure that the slopes are not too steep. A berm may consist solely of high-quality topsoil, but it is more cost effective to use just 1 ft. of high-quality topsoil to cap well-drained subsoil, which can make up the remainder, and the majority, of the berm. Do not construct a berm directly under mature trees, as it will impact those trees negatively.

HOW TO BUILD A BERM

1 Remove the turf from the area where the berm will be placed. Do not berm under established trees or on top of tree roots.

2 Dig up the soil lightly to break up its surface before bringing in additional soil to create the berm.

3 Bring in fill or subsoil to make up the major portion of berm. The slope and shape of the subsoil or fill layer should be developed before the topsoil layer is added.

4 After the subsoil shape is established, first spread a 2–3 inch layer of topsoil and fork it in well. Then add the rest of the topsoil.

5 Spread out a layer of topsoil on top of the subsoil layer. The surfaces of the layers should be parallel—that is, the topsoil thickness should be consistent.

6 Tamp the soil down lightly and smooth the slopes with the back of a rake.

7 Plant the berm with trees and shrubs.

Vinnie's Top Fifteen Screening Plants

APPENDIX 1

This list is a sincere attempt to present my top fifteen select screening plants for the garden. These plants were chosen for their aesthetic value, fast growth, adaptability, and exceptional function in the landscape, all virtues required of an effective screening plant. Both evergreen and deciduous woody plants are represented here. Plants with the letters "DR" after them have shown moderate to good deer resistance in the landscape.

1. Western arborvitae (*Thuja plicata*) DR
2. Oriental spruce (*Picea orientalis*)
3. Japanese cryptomeria (*Cryptomeria japonica*)
4. Inkberry holly (*Ilex glabra*)
5. Leatherleaf viburnum (*Viburnum rhytidophyllum*)
6. Cutleaf stephanandra (*Stephanandra incisa*)
7. Cherry laurel (*Prunus laurocerasus*)
8. Plum Yew (*Cephalotaxus harringtonia*) DR
9. White fir (*Abies concolor*)
10. Border forsythia (*Forsythia × intermedia*)
11. Chinese loropetalum (*Loropetalum chinense*)
12. Lawson falsecypress (*Chamaecyparis lawsoniana*)
13. Lacebark pine (*Pinus bungeana*)

14. Japanese pieris (*Pieris japonica*) DR

15. Japanese privet (*Ligustrum japonicum*)

Gardens Worth Visiting

APPENDIX 2

One of the best ways to learn about plants is to visit your local public garden. These educational institutions provide magnificent gardens and offer useful information about some of your favorite woody plants. For gardeners who are in the market for new evergreens or other screening plants, visiting the local public garden can prove to be very valuable when designing your garden. Whether researching for your own garden or just visiting to appreciate their sheer beauty, public gardens can be a valuable resource. Below is a listing of a few of my favorite public gardens.

Atlanta Botanical Garden
1345 Piedmont Avenue NE
Atlanta, GA 30309
www.atlantabotanicalgarden.org/home.do

Bayard Cutting Arboretum
440 Montauk Highway
Great River, NY 11739
Mailing address P.O. Box 466
Oakdale, NY 11769
www.bayardcuttingarboretum.com

Biltmore Estate
1 Approach Road
Asheville, NC 28803
www.biltmore.com

Botanic Garden of Smith College
College Lane
Northampton, MA 01063
www.smith.edu/garden/home.html

Brooklyn Botanic Garden
1000 Washington Avenue
Brooklyn, NY 11225
http://bbg.org

Chicago Botanic Garden
1000 Lake Cook Road
Glencoe, IL 60022
www.chicagobotanic.org

Cornell Plantations
One Plantations Road
Ithaca, NY 14850
www.plantations.cornell.edu
   Clement Gray Bowers
   Rhododendron Collection
   www.plantations.cornell.edu/collections/
   botanical/rhodo.cfm
   Deans Garden
   www.plantations.cornell.edu/collections/
   botanical/deans.cfm
   Mullestein Winter Garden
   www.plantations.cornell.edu/collections/
   botanical/winter.cfm
   F. R. Newman Arboretum
   www.plantations.cornell.edu/collections/
   arboretum.cfm
   Zucker Shrub Sampler,
   Newman Arboretum
   www.plantations.cornell.edu/collections/
   botanical/shrub.cfm

Hofstra Arboretum
Hofstra University
Hempstead, NY 11549-1000
www.hofstra.edu/COM/Arbor/index_Arbor.cfm

Holden Arboretum
9500 Sperry Road
Kirtland, OH 44094
www.holdenarb.org

Lewis Ginter Botanical Garden
1800 Lakeside Avenue
Richmond, VA 23228-4700
www.lewisginter.org

Longwood Gardens
1001 Longwood Road
Kennett Square, PA 19348
www.longwoodgardens.org

Missouri Botanic Garden
4344 Shaw Boulevard
St. Louis, MO 63110
www.mobot.org

Morton Arboretum
4100 Illinois Route 53
Lisle, IL 60532-1293
www.mortonarb.org

Mount Auburn Cemetery
580 Mount Auburn Street
Cambridge, MA 02138
www.mountauburn.org

New York Botanical Garden
Bronx River Parkway
at Fordham Road
Bronx, NY 10458
http://nybg.org

Old Westbury Gardens
71 Old Westbury Road
P.O. Box 430
Old Westbury, NY 11568
www.oldwestburygardens.org

Phipps Conservatory and Botanical Gardens
One Schenley Park
Pittsburgh, PA 15213-3830
www.phipps.conservatory.org

Planting Fields Arboretum State Historic Park and Coe Hall
1395 Planting Fields Road
Oyster Bay, NY 11771
www.plantingfields.org

Scott Arboretum
of Swarthmore College
500 College Avenue
Swarthmore, PA 19081
www.scottarboretum.org

United States Botanical Garden
245 First Street, SW
Washington, DC 20024
www.usbg.gov

United States National Arboretum
3501 New York Avenue, NE
Washington, DC 20002-1958
www.usna.usda.gov

University of Wisconsin–Madison Arboretum
1207 Seminole Highway
Madison, WI 53711-3726
http://uwarboretum.org

Winterthur Museum & Country Estate
Route 52 (Kennett Pike)
Winterthur, DE 19735
www.winterthur.org

Boxwood and yew in a formal English garden

APPENDIX 3

The internet can be a very valuable resource when trying to locate evergreen and shrubs for your landscape. This is especially true of new and unusual or even rare plant varieties that are difficult to find. Many mail-order nurseries and garden supply companies provide excellent, select horticultural materials and plants for home gardeners. Below is a listing of some exceptional mail-order nurseries and helpful Web sites.

Broken Arrow Nursery
13 Broken Arrow Road
Hamden, CT 06518
www.brokenarrownursery.com

Camellia Forest Nursery
9701 Carrie Road
Chapel Hill, NC 27516
www.camforest.com

Collector's Nursery
16804 NE 102nd Avenue
Battle Ground, Washington 98604
www.collectorsnursery.com

Cornell Cooperative Extension: Gardening Cornell University
Ithaca, NY 14853
http://www.gardening.cornell.edu/index.html

Fairweather Gardens
P.O. Box 330
Greenwich, NJ 08323
www.fairweathergardens.com

Forestfarm
990 Tetherow Road
Williams, OR 97544-9599
www.forestfarm.com

Gardener's Supply Company
128 Intervale Road
Burlington, VT 05401-2804
www.gardeners.com

Gossler Farms Nursery
1200 Weaver Road
Springfield, OR 97478
www.gosslerfarms.com

Greer Gardens
1280 Goodpasture Island Road
Eugene, OR 97401-1755
www.greergardens.com

Heronswood Nursery
300 Park Avenue
Warminster, PA 18974
www.heronswood.com

Meadowbrook Nursery: We-Du Natives
2055 Polly Spout Road
Marion, NC 28752
www.we-du.com

Niche Gardens
1111 Dawson Road
Chapel Hill, NC 27516
www.nichegardens.com

Plant Delights Nursery, Inc.
9241 Sauls Road
Raleigh, NC 27603
www.plantdelights.com

RareFind Nursery
957 Patterson Road
Jackson, NJ 08527
www.rarefindnursery.com

**Rhododendron Species Foundation
and Botanical Garden**
2525 South 336th Street
Federal Way, WA 98003
Mailing address P.O. Box 3798
Federal Way, WA 98063
www.rhodygarden.org

Siskyou Rare Plant Nursery
2115 Talent Avenue
Talent, OR 97540
www.srpn.net

**Song Sparrow Perennial Farm
and Nursery**
13101 E. Rye Road
Avalon, WI 53505
www.songsparrow.com

Woodlanders, Inc.
1128 Colleton Avenue
Aiken, SC 29801
www.woodlanders.net

Accent. An attractive-looking tree or shrub that will add interest to the garden. An accent plant can offer interesting bark, contrasting foliage, flowers, or fruit and brighten up the landscape. An example is a tree with variegated foliage that livens up a shady area of the garden.

Anti-desiccant. A product applied to plant foliage to reduce water loss.

Balled and burlapped. A method of supporting and protecting the roots of a transplanted tree or shrub.

Berm. A raised area of the garden used to elevate a planting bed or provide privacy in the garden.

Biological control. Controlling harmful pests with beneficial organisms.

Broadleaf evergreen. A woody plant with wider leaves than those of a needled evergreen.

Canopy. Collective foliage created by the leaves of trees and shrubs.

Chemical control. Controlling pests with chemical pesticides.

Compost. Rich, organic material comprising humus and other organic material and used to improve soil conditions.

Conifer. A cone-bearing plant having thin, needlelike leaves.

Cultivated variety, *also known as a cultivar or garden variety.* A variation of a species that is produced through breeding or selection. A cultivated variety is most often of garden origin.

Cultural control. Controlling pests with cultural practices such as sanitation and crop rotation.

Culture. Environmental factors that govern the success of any given plant such as soil, light and water needs.

Cutback shrub. A shrub that is severely pruned annually or every few years in early spring to promote new, vigorous vegetative growth and/or flowers.

Deciduous. Shedding leaves at the end of the growing season and regaining them in spring the next growing season.

Dioecious. With male and female flowers confined to separate plants. Holly is an example of a dioecious shrub.

Evergreen. A plant that retains its leaves year-round.

Foundation planting. A planting used near the foundation of a house or other structure to add an ornamental feature or soften architectural lines.

Grouping. A small number of strategically placed trees and shrubs that achieve a harmonious look and function. If room is limited and a large quantity of trees and shrubs is not necessary, a smaller grouping will maintain harmony on a reduced scale. Groupings in odd numbers, such as three, five, or seven, can provide a less formal, natural look.

Hedge. A formal or informal planting that blocks or separates one area of the garden from another or defines a property line.

Humus. A naturally complex organic material made up of plant matter or animal manure.

Leaf margin. The edge of a leaf.

Mass planting. Using one type of tree or shrub in significant quantities will create harmony and maximize the effect these plants can have in the landscape. A mass planting is meant to create a natural rhythm that is pleasing to the eye and is often more attractive than one tree or shrub planted alone. A mass planting is also meant to be seen from a distance and can provide additional function as a barrier or living screen.

Mechanical control. Using tools or machinery to remove harmful pests, including invasive weeds.

Mulch. A layer of material, usually organic, applied to the soil surface to suppress weeds, retain soil moisture, moderate soil temperature, and add organic matter to the soil.

Needle. A thin leaf blade.

Neutral soil. Soil with a pH of 7.0.

pH. The measure of soil alkalinity or acidity. Soil pH is measured on a scale from 1 to 14, with 1 being the most acidic and 14 being the most alkaline. A pH reading of 7 is considered neutral.

Physical control. Physically removing harmful pests from plants.

Pot-bound. A root system that has crowded a pot and occupies the majority of the soil in a container.

Rejuvenative (or rejuvenation) pruning. Severely pruning a plant while dormant to encourage a flush or new spring growth.

Root-ball. The root system of a plant usually associated with a transplant.

Root flare. The swollen area of a plant near the base.

Screening. When shrubs or trees function as a physical and visual barrier in the landscape. The purpose of screening is to hide a specific view, create privacy, or even act as a buffer to wind or noise. Evergreens or densely branched upright shrubs should be selected for this purpose and used en masse.

Selective pruning. A method of pruning where select stems are removed from a plant to improve plant health, flower, or fruit production and overall appearance.

Shearing. The removal of a plant's surface growth by clipping in order to achieve a desired shape.

Specimen planting. Usually, an individual plant that is very noticeable and is featured as a stand-alone plant in the landscape. A strategically placed plant specimen can be considered a focal point or even the main attraction in the garden. In a large garden, several specimens of the same species may be clumped together in a grouping to create a bolder impact.

Subsoil. The soil layer beneath topsoil layer.

Topsoil. The soil at the surface of the earth, wherein plants are grown. It is the soil with the most organic matter in it.

Understory. An underlying layer of vegetation, specifically the vegetative layer and especially the trees and shrubs between the forest canopy and the groundcover.

Variegation. Striping, edging, or other marking with a color different from the primary color. Variegated foliage can have creamy white, gold, or other showy colors contrasting with the basic green.

Variety. A naturally occurring subdivision of a species, having distinct and sometimes inconspicuous differences and breeding true to those differences. Different from cultivated variety.

Winter burn. Damage to plant foliage usually from cold temperatures, sunlight and wind in the winter.

Woody plant. Any vascular plant that has a stem that is aboveground and covered by a layer of thickened, woody bark. Woody plants are usually trees, shrubs, or perennial vines.

Hedge display showing an assortment of hedging plants

Bibliography

In addition to the websites listed in the "Noteworthy Mail-order Nurseries and Helpful Websites" section, other websites and books were used in gathering the information for Great Landscape Evergreens.

Bailey Hortorium. *Hortus Third*. New York: Macmillan, 1976.

bestgardening.com. *Design Basics: Hedges*. Christchurch, New Zealand, 2001. http://www.bestgardening.com/ bgc/design/designbasicshedges01.htm.

Better Homes and Gardens. *New Complete Guide to Landscaping*. Des Moines, Iowa: Meredith Books, 2002.

Booth, Norman K., and James E. Hiss. *Residential Landscape Architecture*, 2nd ed. Englewood Cliffs, N.J.: Prentice Hall, 1999.

Brand, Mark. *UConn Plant Database of Trees, Shrubs and Vines*. Storrs, Conn.: University of Connecticut, 2001. http://www.hort.uconn.edu/plants/.

Brooks, Dick. "The Weston Hybrids." *Journal of the American Rhododendron Society* 53, no. 4 (1999): 195. Also available online at http://www.rhododendron.org/v53n4p195.htm.

Cornell Cooperative Extension of Nassau County. *Horticulture Fact Sheets*. East Meadow, NY: Author, 2007. http://www.ccenassau.org/hort/html/fact_sheets_home_hort.html.

Dave's Garden. *Gardenology*. Bryan / College Station, Tex.: Author, 2007. http://davesgarden.com/terms/.

Dirr, Michael A. *Dirr's Hardy Trees and Shrubs*, 5th ed. Portland, OR: Timber Press, 1997.

———. *Manual of Woody Landscape Plants: Their Identification, Ornamental Characteristics, Culture, Propagation and Uses*, 5th ed. Champaign, Ill.: Stipes, 1998.

Evans, Erv. *Plant Fact Sheets*. Raleigh: NC State University, 2005. http://www.ces.ncsu.edu/depts/hort/consumer/ factsheets/.

Farlex. *TheFreeDictionary*. Huntingdon Valley, Penn.: Author, 2007. http://www.thefreedictionary.com/garden.

Good, G. L., and R. Weir. *The Cornell Guide for Planting and Maintaining Trees and Shrubs*. Ithaca, N.Y.: Cornell University Resource Center, 2005.

Hillier Nurseries. *The Hillier Manual of Trees and Shrubs*, 8th ed. Newton Abbot, England: David & Charles, 2002.

Jauron, Richard. "Selecting and Planting Hedges." *Horticulture and Home Pest News* (March 31, 1995): 34. Updated by John VanDyk. Ames: Iowa State University, 1998. Available online at http://www.ipm.iastate.edu/ipm/hort-news/1995/3-31-1995/hedge.html.

Kelly, John, ed. *The Hillier Gardener's Guide to Trees and Shrubs*. Pleasantville, N.Y.: Reader's Digest, 1997.

Michigan State University Extension. *Chamaecyparis thyoides—Whitecedar Falsecypress*. East Lansing, Mich.: Author, 2000. http://web1.msue.msu.edu/imp/modzz/00000342.html.

Rakow, Donald A., and Richard Weir III. *Pruning: An Illustrated Guide to Pruning Ornamental Trees and Shrubs*. Ithaca, N.Y.: Cornell Cooperative Extension, 2005. Downloadable through http://hdl.handle.net/1813/3573.

Starbuck, Christopher J. Selecting Landscape Plants: Needled Evergreens. University of Missouri Extension. http://extension.missouri.edu/explore/agguides/hort/g06815.htm.

Stephen F. Austin State University SFA Mast Arboretum. Loropetalum chinense *var.* rubrum *'Burgundy': Chinese Fringe-flower*. Nacogdoches, Tex.: Author. http://arboretum.sfasu.edu/plants/loropetalumchinense/index.htm.

Shaughnessy, Debbie, and Bob Polomski. *Leyland Cypress*. Clemson, S.C.: Clemson University Cooperative Extension Service, 1999. http://hgic.clemson.edu/factsheets/HGIC1013.htm.

University of Delaware Botanic Gardens. Chamaecyparis lawsoniana. Newark, Del.: Author, 2006. http://ag.udel.edu/udbg/conifers/c_lawsoniana.html.

Wilkins, Susan, and Kathleen Bennett. *Building Soil Berms*. Sustainable Urban Landscape Information Series. St. Paul: University of Minnesota, 2006. http://www.sustland.umn.edu/implement/soil_berms.html.

United States Air Force. "Landscape Design." In *USAF Landscape Design Guide*. 1998. http://www.afcee.brooks.af.mil/ldg/s01LandscapeDesign/c03LandscapePlanning.html.

Wikipedia: The Free Encyclopedia. http://en.wikipedia.org/wiki/Main_Page.

Index of Scientific Plant Names

Index of Common Plant Names

Vincent A. Simeone

Vincent has worked in the horticultural field for over twenty years. He has degrees from Farmingdale State University, the University of Georgia, and the C. W. Post Campus of Long Island University. Vincent has specialized expertise in woody plant identification, plant culture, landscape use, and selection of superior varieties. Vincent is also an experienced lecturer, instructor, and horticultural consultant. He continues to promote innovative trends in gardening, such as proper plant selection, four-season gardening, integrated pest management, and low-maintenance gardening.

Vincent teaches a diverse assortment of gardening classes and has assisted in special garden tours to many beautiful gardens in Canada, southern England, northern France, southern Germany, Ireland, New Zealand, and South Africa. Vincent is also very active in the community on local, regional, and national levels with garden clubs, horticultural trade associations, and public garden organizations. Vincent currently works in public horticulture, managing Planting Fields Arboretum State Historic Park in Oyster Bay, New York.

Vincent A. Simeone and Pickles

Bruce Curtis

Bruce has chronicled many of the significant events of the last decades of the twentieth century as a photographer for *Time*,

Bruce Curtis

LIFE, and *Sports Illustrated*. He has been on the front lines of the Vietnam War, covered the explorations of Jacques Cousteau, captured the glory of the Papal Archives, and chronicled the action on the fast-paced sports field.

His uncanny ability to capture the significant moment led Bruce to explore special effects with MIT electrical engineering professor and strobe photography pioneer Dr. Harold Edgerton. Bruce's interest in action photography inspired him to use pyrotechnics and laser light to create the "action still life," a combination of the best of special effects and still life photography in one dynamic image. The demand for his images in posters, calendars, books, greeting cards, and CD-ROMs continues to grow. Bruce's studio is located on Long Island, New York.